T5-AFL-243

THE DECREE ON THE PASTORAL OFFICE OF BISHOPS IN THE CHURCH

Christus Dominus

THE DECREE ON THE PASTORAL OFFICE OF BISHOPS IN THE CHURCH

Commentary
by
WILLY ONCLIN

VATICAN II DOCUMENTS
PAULIST PRESS
Glen Rock, New Jersey

The Commentary by Willy Onclin was translated by Joseph A. Horn. The text of the Decree was translated by Redmond Fitzmaurice, O.P.

NIHIL OBSTAT:
Rev. James J. O'Connor
Censor Librorum

IMPRIMATUR:
✠ Leo A. Pursley, D.D.
Bishop of Fort Wayne-South Bend

July 3, 1967

Library of Congress
Catalog Card Number: 67-28693

Published by Paulist Press
Editorial Office: 304 W. 58th St., N.Y., N.Y. 10019
Business Office: Glen Rock, New Jersey 07452

**Printed and bound in the
United States of America
by Our Sunday Visitor Press**

Contents

Commentary

INTRODUCTION

Origin, Title and Structure of the Decree

I. Historical Survey of the Origin of the Decree[1]

During the preparatory period for the Council, the Commission on Bishops and the Government of Dioceses, which was presided over first by Cardinal M. Mimmi and then, after his death, by Cardinal P. Marella, was given the task of drawing up seven schemas for decrees.

These schemas were entitled: (1) "On Relations between the Bishops and the Congregations of the Roman Curia"; (2) "On the Division of Dioceses"; (3) "On Coadjutor and Auxiliary Bishops and the Resignation of Bishops from Their Pastoral Office"; (4) "On the Council or Conference of Bishops"; (5) "On Relations between Bishops and Priests"; (6) "On Relations between Bishops and Religious, Especially concerning the Works

[1] On this subject cf. also P. Veuillot, "Introduction au décret sur la charge pastorale des évêques dans l'Eglise," in *Documents conciliaires,* 2 (Paris: Editions du Centurion, 1965), pp. 15-18.

of the Apostolate"; (7) "Important Questions concerning the Care of Souls." This last schema, the most important of all, consisted of two parts: "The Care of Souls in General", treating pastoral problems in general, and "The Care of Souls in Particular", dealing with pastoral duties relating to certain groups of the faithful—namely, emigrants, seamen, airplane personnel, nomads and tourists, as well as Christians exposed to Marxist influences. At the request of the Central Commission, this schema had to be further abridged and combined with other schemas relating to similar matters. Therefore the Commission on Bishops, with the help of the secretaries and some experts from other preparatory commissions, prepared certain propositions resulting from the combining of the various schemas. Finally the Central Subcommission for Mixed Matters composed an even shorter revision of the schema; entitled "On the Care of Souls", it was published in 1962 in the third series of schemas of constitutions and decrees.

After the long and often arduous deliberations and discussions that took place during the first session of the Council (from October 11 to December 8, 1962), it became clear that the Council simply could not take up all the schemas prepared by the preparatory commissions and now in the hands of the Central Commission. The Council could not run on indefinitely without causing grave harm to the various dioceses because of the prolonged and repeated absences of their pastors. Thus the proposed schemas had to be abridged even further.

Toward the end of the first session of the Council, the Council fathers were given a detailed index of the twenty schemas of constitutions and decrees, among which were chosen the questions to be submitted to the Council. Among these schemas were

"On Bishops and the Government of Dioceses" and "On the Care of Souls", each comprising several questions. However, a communication from the commission in charge of coordinating the work of the Council directed the various commissions to make a choice from among the questions indicated for each schema and to keep only the most important ones and those pertaining to the universal Church and Christianity or all mankind. This communication also specified that the schemas must include only general principles relating to these questions, leaving particular problems to be handled by the Commission for the Revision of the Code of Canon Law.

To carry out these directives, the cardinal president of the councilar Commission on Bishops and the Government of Dioceses instructed a lower commission composed of members and experts from the aforesaid commission to draw up a new schema "On Bishops and the Government of Dioceses". He gave another lower commission the task of rewriting the schema "On the Care of Souls". The work of revising the schema "On Bishops and the Government of Dioceses" was finished at the beginning of March, 1963. The new schema was forwarded to the cardinal president of the Coordinating Commission on March 12 of the same year and sent to the members and experts of the Commission on Bishops. The latter were requested to present any remarks they might want to make relative to the schema before the end of June. The new schema was studied and amended once more on May 3 by a lower commission composed of some members of the counciliar commission.

The schema "On Bishops and the Government of Dioceses", as finally printed and submitted for discussion to the Council fathers, was very brief and treated only a few questions concerning bishops. In its five chapters, it (1) set forth certain principles concerning the relationships between bishops and the Roman congregations; (2) defined briefly the status of coadjutor and auxiliary bishops; (3) established certain rules regarding national conferences of bishops (the constitution, administration and competence of these conferences); (4) stated certain principles concerning the division of dioceses; (5) gave general directives regarding the establishment and division of parishes. Thus this schema did not deal at all with the mission of the bishops as the successors of the apostles in the Church of Christ, or with the task that they have to fulfill in that Church, or with the powers with which they are invested.

The schema "On the Care of Souls" was also divided into five chapters containing a certain number of principles and norms on various pastoral questions: (1) the pastoral office of bishops; (2) the pastoral duty of priests; (3) the relationships between bishops and religious, especially concerning the works of the apostolate; (4) pastoral care regarding certain particular groups of the faithful; (5) the catechetical formation of the Christian people. To this schema were added seven appendices in which the principles of the schema were explained and applied, but which were not to be submitted to the approval of the Council fathers.

The schema "On the Care of Souls" was never discussed in the aula of the Council. The schema "On Bishops and the Government of Dioceses", however, was discussed by the Council fathers during the third session, in November, 1963, and provoked some lively criticism. The bishops had hoped to find in it a thorough treatment of the entire mission of the bishops in the Church of Christ. As some of them remarked, the bishops had expected that Vatican Council II, with its widely publicized pastoral and ecumenical purpose, would issue a declaration on the pastoral duties of the bishops which would at least establish basic principles concerning the place of the bishops in the Church, the task which they had to fulfill and the powers which they possessed. Such a thorough treatment seemed particularly necessary to them since no council as a whole had ever defined the mission of the bishops in the Church, and since the definitions of Vatican Council I, which determined the powers and prerogatives in the Church belonging to the sovereign pontiff and constituted a charta for the papacy, demanded as a necessary complement a declaration on the mission and competence of the bishops in the same Church of Christ—a declaration which would constitute a charta for the episcopacy. Besides, as some speakers remarked, reasons of an ecumenical order made it imperative that the role of the bishops in the Church be defined. Finally, certain fathers advised that the decree on bishops should include several pastoral directives contained in the schema "On the Care of Souls".

Consequently the Commission on Bishops and the Government of Dioceses found it necessary to entirely rework the schema "On Bishops and the Government of Dioceses" and to draw up a new and improved plan for the schema. Thus, on November 20, in a meeting of the presidents and secretaries of the five subcommissions already established for the Council, the cardinal president of the commission issued instructions concerning the work of revising the schema to be done in the various subcommissions, as well as directives indicating how this was to be carried out. The first subcommission, which had been put in charge of the new revision of the schema, held meetings on November 25 and 28 and determined the plan of work and the method to be followed.

In a letter on November 29, the Coordinating Commission of the Council instructed the Commission on Bishops to revise the text of the schema in line with the suggestions of the Council fathers. Consequently the lower commission, consisting of chairmen and secretaries, met again on December 3. It was decided to study carefully all the remarks and proposals made by the Council fathers and to meet again in Rome at the close of January to decide the procedure to be followed in revising the schema and to study the possibility of combining the decrees "On Bishops and the Government of Dioceses" and "On the Care of Souls" into one decree.

Meanwhile, on December 18, 1963, the cardinal president of the Commission on Bishops sent a letter to the Coordinating Commission asking the latter to decide on the possibility and advisability of combining the two decrees just mentioned. On January 23, 1964, the cardinal president of the Coordinating Commission informed the president of the Commission on Bishops of the decision made by the Coordinating Commission in this matter. According to the terms of this decision, the schema "On Bishops and the Government of Dioceses" was to include both the most significant norms and the most important directives of the schema "On the Care of Souls"; the latter schema as such was no longer to appear on the list of schemas to be considered by the Council. In the new revision of the schema, which was drawn up in keeping with this decision, there was ample opportunity to fulfill the directives already laid down on March 26, 1963, which stipulated that the matters contained in the schemas were to be treated in accord with the primarily pastoral purpose of Vatican Council II, while questions of a juridical nature were to be left to the Commission on the Revision of the Code of Canon Law.

On January 27, 1964, at the meeting of the lower commission of chairmen and secretaries from the five subcommissions, a new plan for the schema, which had been drawn up on the meantime and submitted to the meeting by the representatives of the first subcommission, was accepted as a basis of discussion of the new enlarged schema, to be entitled "On the Pastoral Office of Bishops in the Church". According to this plan, the schema was divided into a preface and three chapters. The preface described in a general way the mission entrusted to the bishops by Christ, and the three chapters took up in order the mission of the bishops with regard to the universal Church, the pastoral task of each bishop in the particular Church entrusted to his care, and finally the mission attributed jointly to many bishops regarding different Churches taken as a whole. It was within the framework of this plan that, throughout the days that followed, the aforesaid lower commission worked out a schema which was forwarded to all the members of the conciliar Commission on Bishops on January 13, 1964. This commission, which met in Rome on March 3, 1964, to study the new schema, gave its approval to the plan and, after making certain changes in the text, reached final agreement on its formulation on March 13. The schema which resulted from these labors was sent on to the Coordinating Commission a few days later. In a meeting on April 16, the latter commission received the schema favorably and ordered it to be printed and forwarded to the Council fathers immediately. It was also decided to restrict any debate on this schema in the general assemblies of the Council to the texts borrowed from the schema "On the Care of Souls" and those texts which had not yet been discussed in the Council. After a meeting of the lower commission of chairmen and secretaries on April 27 and 28, the schema was given the final touches and then printed and sent to the bishops on May 22, 1964.

Thus the discussion during the general assemblies of the third session of the Council dealt only with those parts which were new and which had not yet been the subject of conciliar debates. In general the new schema was favorably received by the Council assembly, although certain fathers did express objections and propose amendments.

Then the Commission on Bishops proceeded to revise the text anew, correcting it according to the amendments it considered pertinent. It was also admitted that a rather substantial change in the text concerning the mission of the bishops in the universal Church should be made. For the text proposed in the schema, it substituted a text borrowed from the *Dogmatic Constitution on the Church* (*Lumen gentium*). However, only that passage of this Constitution which described the power of the college of bishops as supreme was reproduced in the amended schema, while another passage of the same Constitution which referred to this power as full and supreme was not repeated in the revised schema. It was chiefly because of this omission, which could have led to a great deal of misunderstanding, that Chapter I of the schema did not obtain the necessary two-thirds vote in the Council. In the vote taken on this entire chapter (on November 4, 1964), although only 77 rejected the text by voting *non placet,* 852 votes *placet juxta modum* were accompanied by amendments, particularly in regard to nn. 4 and 8 of the chapter. The text of Chapter II was put to a vote and likewise did not obtain the two-thirds vote required for approval, chiefly because the treatment of coadjutor and auxiliary bishops and the statements concerning the relationships between diocesan bishops and religious were not entirely satisfactory. There were only 19 votes *non placet,* but 889 votes *placet juxta modum* brought in new amendments. Chapter III of the schema, on the other hand, was passed by the majority of those voting in the same assembly on November 6.

Then the commission took up the task of revising the text and working in the amendments proposed by a considerable number of the fathers. Thus amended, the schema was submitted to the vote of the fathers during the fourth session of the Council. This time it obtained the required majority. On November 6, 1965, the entire schema was passed by the conciliar assembly by a vote of 2,167 to 14.

Finally, in the public session on November 18, 1965, the text was put to a vote again, in the presence of the sovereign pontiff, and received practically unanimous approval from the Council fathers. There were only two dissenting votes. The schema "On the Pastoral Office of Bishops in the Church" was approved by the sovereign pontiff, who ordered it to be promulgated and decreed that it should go into effect on June 29, 1966.[2] These eight months of *vacatio legis* were certainly needed to finish drawing up the measures by which the various particulars of the Decree were to be carried out. This period

---

[2] The Decree *Christus Dominus* (*De pastorali Episcoporum munere in Ecclesia*) was promulgated in *A.A.S.* 58 (1966), pp. 673-701.

of time proved to be insufficient. Consequently, the *vacatio legis* was extended by the Motu Proprio *Munus apostolicum* of June 10, 1966, which declared that the term of the *vacatio* would be determined for each decree by a separate pronouncement.[3] These pronouncements were not long in coming. On June 15, 1966, the Motu Proprio *De episcoporum muneribus*, which put into effect n. 8b of the Decree, promulgated the list of universal laws of the Church which in principle could be dispensed from only by the Holy See.[4] According to the terms of the Motu Proprio, the regulations of the decree *Christus Dominus* concerning the power of dispensing granted to diocesan bishops were to go into effect on August 15, 1966. The measures for carrying out the other prescriptions of this Decree were issued on August 6 in the Motu Proprio *Ecclesiae sanctae* [5] and were to go into effect on October 11, 1966. These measures were primarily concerned with the appointments of priests, a matter dealt with in Chapter I, n. 6 of the Decree. They also treated the many prescriptions of Chapter II—namely, pastoral study and knowledge, the equitable remuneration to be guaranteed to sacred ministers, particular care for certain groups of the faithful, the appointment of bishops, the resignation of episcopal office by a bishop, the division of dioceses, the powers of auxiliary bishops, episcopal vicars, priests' senates and pastoral councils, the suppression of rights and privileges concerning the

---

[3] Pope Paul VI, Motu Proprio *Munus apostolicum*, June 10, 1966: *A.A.S.* 58 (1966), pp. 465-66.

[4] Pope Paul VI, Motu Proprio *De episcoporum muneribus*, setting forth norms by which bishops may grant dispensations, June 15, 1966: *A.A.S.* 58 (1966), pp. 467-72.

[5] Pope Paul VI, Motu Proprio *Ecclesiae sanctae*, August 6, 1966: *L'Osservatore Romano*, August 13, 1966, pp. 1-2.

bestowal of ecclesiastical offices, rural vicars or deans, the transfer and resignation of pastors, the erection and suppression of parishes and innovations relative to these matters, and the relationships between bishops and religious. The instruction concluded with a treatment of certain prescriptions of Chapter III, particularly in regard to episcopal conferences, the division of ecclesiastical provinces and regions, and, finally, the revision of pastoral directives.

II. The Title of the Decree

1. Decree on the Pastoral Office of Bishops in the Church: Such is the designation of this Council document. First of all it is called a *Decree.* Certainly the document recalls the doctrinal foundations underlying the mission of the bishops in the Church. Nevertheless, its most important purpose is not to establish the theological doctrine concerning the mission of the bishops (a task already accomplished in the Dogmatic Constitution *Lumen gentium*), but rather to draw from this doctrine some conclusions concerning the pastoral office which the bishops have to fulfill both in the universal Church and in the particular Churches which are entrusted to them and in which they must make present the Church of Christ. In a way, then, this document amounts to a practical application of the doctrine contained in *Lumen gentium,* and it is intended to give directives for the carrying out of this mission. That is why it is rightly called a Decree and not a Constitution.

2. The Pastoral Office of Bishops in the Church: This simple title, expressed in general terms, gives a good indication of the entire subject matter of the Decree. In fact the original title of the Decree—"On Bishops and the Government of Dioceses"—no longer corresponded to the contents of this document as willed by the Council fathers. This first title indicated a statement solely, or at least principally, concerned with the office of bishops in the government of the dioceses entrusted to their care. However, the title simply could not be retained once the Council fathers had expressed the wish that the Decree deal with the mission of the bishops considered under its various aspects and in the various activities which it entailed in the Church. Thus the present title, which is more general, corresponds to the wishes of the Council fathers and indicates a complete treatment of the pastoral office which bishops are appointed to fulfill in the Church of Christ.

It may seem strange that, under the general title of the pastoral office of bishops, the Decree considers the pastoral function entailed in this office, as well as the functions of teaching and sanctifying. As a matter of fact, in analyzing the mission proper to the bishops and determining the various functions which this implies, the Decree distinguishes three functions: (1) teaching, which the bishops have to carry out in their role as *fidei magistri*, teachers of the faith; (2) sanctifying, which they must fulfill as *pontifices;* (3) directing or governing, which is the pastoral function in the narrowest sense of the term, and which the bishops carry out as *pastores* or *rectores*. Nevertheless, the entire mission of the bishops in the Church can be called a pastoral mission since every work which they are called to undertake, whether it be teaching, sanctifying or ruling, is essentially pastoral, inasmuch as it is directed to the service of souls.

3. Christus Dominus (Christ the Lord): These

are the first words of the Decree, and therefore the words by which it will be known throughout the history of the Church. Although the words may not have been chosen for any particular reason, nevertheless they do in fact proclaim that the mission under discussion in the Decree—the mission of the bishops, the successors of the apostles—was defined by Christ himself and is therefore a mission of divine right. Surely it is Christ himself who sent the apostles, and who therefore today sends the bishops, their successors, to continue the work of redeeming and sanctifying the men whom the Father entrusted to him: "As the Father has sent me, I also send you" (Jn. 20, 21). It is certainly true that the Church has further specified the ways in which the mission is to be carried out, that mission which the bishops now accomplish under the supreme authority of the sovereign pontiff, the successor of Peter. But it is still Christ himself who gives the bishops their mission. And it is this mission, such as Christ confers it and the Church further defines it, that is treated by the present Decree.

III. Structure of the Decree—The Preface

The *Decree on the Pastoral Office of Bishops in the Church* is divided into three chapters and introduced by a Preface. The latter first of all lays down the foundations of the pastoral duties of the bishops, namely the mission given by Christ to the apostles and thence to the bishops, their successors. It also shows the organic unity of the Decree by explaining the division into three chapters.

(a) It is the mission conferred by Christ that constitutes the foundation of the pastoral task proper to the bishops. Starting with the idea that this divine mission was conferred on the apostles (n. 1), the Preface states first of all that in the Church, as willed and established by her founder, the sovereign pontiff, Peter's successor in the primacy, holds supreme, full, immediate and universal power, which is to be used for the good of souls. In so doing, it confirms the doctrine defined by Vatican Council I,[6] contained in the Code of Canon Law (Can. 218, §§ 1 and 2), and affirmed once again by the Dogmatic Constitution *Lumen gentium*.[7]

Then the Preface states that, to continue the work of redemption, the bishops themselves were instituted by the Holy Spirit to feed the flock of the Lord (Acts 20, 28). As successors of the apostles, they are constituted pastors of souls, and they are called to continue Christ's work of redemption and sanctification until the end of time in union with the sovereign pontiff and under his authority. The bishops are to accomplish this work by fulfilling the three principal functions of teaching, sanctifying and ruling. Thus the bishops are teachers of the faith, pontiffs and pastors, and they are such by the very nature of the episcopate. In fact all pastoral duties are linked with the episcopate, and the bishops are invested with them by the episcopal consecration itself. Such is the doctrine set forth in *Lumen gentium*, which states: "Episcopal consecration, together with the office of sanctifying, also confers the office of teaching and of governing, which, however, of its very nature, can be exercised only in hierarchical communion with the head and

---

[6] Cf. Vatican Council I, Session 4, Dogmatic Constitution *Pastor aeternus: Denz.* 1821-1822 (3050-3051), 1826-1827 (3054-3055).

[7] Cf. Vatican Council II, Dogmatic Constitution *Lumen gentium*, n. 22: *A.A.S.* 57 (1965), pp. 25-27.

the members of the college."[8] Since the present Decree is so closely joined to this Constitution, it naturally repeats this basic idea.

(b) The *division* of the Decree into three chapters is set forth and explained in n. 3 of the Preface. This division corresponds to the various aspects of the mission which the bishops have in the Church of Christ.

This mission includes first of all the task they have to fulfill in relation to the universal Church and the care they have for the entire Church and for each of the Churches that constitute her. It also includes the task which they have to fulfill in the particular Churches entrusted to their care in a special way. But here we must make a distinction. In principle the bishop in charge of a particular Church, a diocesan bishop, is the only one completely responsible, the only one ensuring the discharge of pastoral duties in that particular church, in that diocese. By way of exception, however, in the matter of pastoral questions for which the good of the particular Church demands a certain uniformity among the various Churches in the same region or country, the bishops in charge of these Churches should work together to fulfill their office toward these churches taken as a group. Thus, in matters pertaining to particular churches, the task of the bishops is carried out in two different ways and consequently must be considered from two different points of view. Therefore the Decree is logically divided into three chapters. The first deals with the duties of bishops in relation to the universal Church. The second spells out the pastoral duties which each bishop is to fulfill individually in the particular Church entrusted to him. Finally, the third chapter establishes certain norms concerning

[8] *Ibid.,* n. 21, pp. 24-25.

the task which several bishops fulfill together in the various individual Churches of the same ecclesiastical province, same region or same country.

The order followed in the Decree is the logical result of the preceding. First of all the Decree determines the office of bishops in the universal Church, presided over by the college of bishops under the authority of the sovereign pontiff. Then it defines the pastoral office which each bishop has to fulfill in the particular Church to which, as a member of the college, he is sent to provide in a special way for the spiritual needs of the faithful who make up that particular church. Finally it establishes certain norms concerning the office which various bishops must fulfill together in the various individual Churches in a given territory.

The order of the different chapters of the Decree was severely criticized by Bishop L. Carli, of Segni, during the discussion in the Council aula. He claimed that this order implied that the first task of the bishops was to care for the entire Church, and he said that he could not accept such a doctrine. In his opinion, the first task of bishops is the care of the particular Churches entrusted to them, and it is that task which forms the basis for the mission they are to fulfill in the universal Church. This viewpoint was not accepted by the Council and is clearly contrary to the doctrine set forth in the Dogmatic Constitution *Lumen gentium*. In fact this Constitution makes it clear [9] that bishops are members of the college of bishops in virtue of the episcopal consecration itself and not in virtue of their assignment to particular Churches. It is because they are members of the college that they can be sent to a particular Church to care for the People of God in that particular area in a special way.

---

[9] *Ibid.*, n. 22, pp. 25-27.

CHAPTER I

BISHOPS AND THE UNIVERSAL CHURCH

Chapter I is divided into two parts. The first part defines the office which the bishops have to fulfill in the universal Church in their capacity as members of the college and the responsibility which they undertake toward the whole Church of Christ and the various individual Churches which comprise it. The second part concerns the relationships between the bishops in charge of particular Churches and the central government of the Church, the Holy See.

I. Role of Bishops in the Universal Church

As members of the college placed in charge of the universal Church, the bishops first of all have the task of participating actively in the entire work which the Church of Christ is doing and in the government thereof by exercising the power of the college of bishops. Their task also includes assisting the supreme pastor of the Church as either chosen or elected members of a supreme council, to be called the "synod of bishops". Finally, bishops are responsible for all the particular Churches which make present and represent the Church of Christ in different parts of the earth.

1. The Exercise of the Power of the College of Bishops (n. 4)

The task of the college of bishops and its responsibility in the work which the universal Church must accomplish were established in the Dogmatic Constitution *Lumen gentium*.[10] The present Decree recalls the essential points of this doctrine and draws conclusions from it.

The college of bishops, to which the bishops belong solely in virtue of episcopal consecration as long as they are in hierarchical communion with the head and members of the college, possesses full and supreme power in the Church of Christ. Of course the sovereign pontiff, the head of the college, also possesses full and supreme power in the universal Church. He is, in fact, a successor in the primacy to Peter, whom the Lord placed in charge of his Church and to whom he gave all the power necessary to fulfill the work which his Church was supposed to do: "And I say to thee, thou art Peter, and upon this rock I will build my Church. . . . And I will give thee the keys of the kingdom of heaven; and whatever thou shalt bind on earth shall be bound in heaven" (Mt. 16, 18). This power of binding and loosing was conferred on Peter by the Lord after his resurrection when he commanded him: "Feed my lambs. . . . Feed my sheep" (Jn. 21, 15-17). But Christ gave this same power of binding and loosing just as surely to the Twelve, the predecessors of the bishops: "Amen I say to you, whatever you bind on earth shall be bound also in heaven; whatever you loose on earth shall be loosed also in heaven" (Mt. 18, 18). He also gave them the mission of teaching the doctrine which he had entrusted to them: "Go, therefore, and make disciples of all nations, baptizing them in the name of the

---

[10] *Ibid.*

Father, and of the Son, and of the Holy Spirit, teaching them to observe all that I have commanded you" (Mt. 28, 19-20). Thus the college of bishops, successor of the apostolic college, in union with the sovereign pontiff, the successor of Peter, also possesses full and supreme power in the Church of Christ.

This full and supreme power is exercised either in an ecumenical council by the bishops assembled together, or outside the council by the bishops scattered throughout the world.

(a) As *Lumen gentium* states, this supreme power is exercised by the college of bishops in a solemn way in an ecumenical council.[11] Recalling the doctrine of this Constitution concerning the ways in which collegial power may be exercised, the present Decree also declares that "this power is solemnly exercised in an ecumenical council". The Decree then draws this conclusion: "Therefore this Council decrees that all bishops who are members of the episcopal college have the right to take part in an ecumenical council." Since they are members of the college of bishops by their consecration, provided they are in communion with the head and members of the college, all consecrated bishops are by right members of the ecumenical council, which is the solemn assembly of the college.

This conclusion arrived at in the Decree introduces a change in the legislation presently in effect in the Code of Canon Law. According to Can. 228, §§ 1 and 2 of the Code, in fact, only those called residential bishops, even if they are not yet consecrated, are called by right to a council. Titular bishops, on the other hand, may be called but do not have to be called. Once called, however, they have a deliberative voice unless the assembly decides otherwise.

---

[11] *Ibid.*

The doctrine contained in the Code of Canon Law had been defended by a large number of canonists. In fact, since the 15th century, the question as to whether titular bishops should be called to an ecumenical council has been the subject of much controversy.

According to one doctrine—the one accepted by the Code—the power of orders on the one hand and the powers of magisterium and jurisdiction on the other are not joined but are independent of one another.[12] A council, in which the bishops are *iudices fidei et morum* ("judges of faith and morals") and therefore exercise not the power of orders but the powers of magisterium and jurisdiction, is by right constituted only by those bishops who possess the power of jurisdiction. Thus, according to the proponents of this doctrine, the only ones who have jurisdiction in the Church are the bishops in charge of particular Churches, and they have jurisdiction even if they have not yet been consecrated as bishops. Since, according to these authors, titular bishops have no power of jurisdiction, they may be called to a council, but need not be. One of the first proponents of this doctrine was Cardinal Dominic Jacobazzi (1443-1527), an ardent defender of pontifical powers, who dealt with this subject in his *Tractatus de Con-*

---

[12] For theories concerning relationships between the power of orders and the episcopal power of jurisdiction, cf. J. Lécuyer, "L'épiscopat selon S. Thomas," in *Etudes sur la Collégialité épiscopale* (Lyons, 1964), pp. 99-101; M. Useros, "Orden y jurisdicción. Tradición teologico-canónica y tradición liturgica primitiva," in *Revista Española de Derecho Canónico* 19 (1964), pp. 689-723; G. Alberigo, "La collegialite épiscopale selon quelques theologiens de la papauté," in *La collégialité épiscopale. Histoire et Théologie* (Unam Sanctam, 52) (Paris, 1965), pp. 183-221, especially pp. 195-221.

cilio.[13] He was followed by a large number of authors, such as Melchior Cano, Fr. Suarez, Fr. Schmalzgrueber, A. J. Andreucci, Ph. de Angelis,[14]

[13] Cardinal Jacobazzi, *Tractatus de Concilio,* Book II, n. 68, in *Tractatus illustrium in utraque tum Pontificii tum Caesaris iuris facultate iurisconsultorum,* Vol. XIII, Part I (Venice, 1584), fol. 212. On the question whether titular bishops must be called to a council, after giving reasons in favor of an affirmative answer, he writes: "But the answer seems to be the opposite, because voting in the council pertains not only to orders but also to jurisdiction. . . . Therefore it follows that, since they cannot have a deliberative voice, they do not have to be called. And it seems the same must be said for bishops who have resigned the episcopacy."

[14] Melchior Cano, *De locis theologicis* (Venice, 1776), Book V, Ch. 2, p. 110, is of the same opinion because "all the affairs of the council are carried out not by the power of orders but by the power of jurisdiction". Thus also F. Suarez, *Tractatus de fide theologica* (*Opera omnia,* Vol. XII [Paris, 1858]), Disp. XI, "De conciliis," Sect. 1, n. 18 (p. 327 in this edition): "Titular bishops may certainly be called to a council and vote there. But *per se* this is not at all necessary since they have no jurisdiction. And that is the present practice." Cf. also F. Schmalzgrueber, *Ius ecclesiaticum universum* (Dillingen, 1719), Vol. I, *Dissertatio prooemialis,* n. 325, p. 132. Also A. J. Andreucci, *Hierarchia ecclesiastica* (Rome, 1776), Book I, Treatise I, "De Episcopo titulari," Part 2, n. 118, p. 47, and n. 122, p. 48: "For all and only those bishops must be called to a council who have Christian people subject to them and who are actually judges of faith and morals. . . . But since titular bishops, for lack of actual subjects (unless they be given them by the pope), are not actually judges of faith and morals, it follows that *per se* they do not have to be called." Also among the authors who favor this theory is L. Ferraris, *Prompta Bibliotheca canonica, iuridica, moralis, theologica,* Vol. II (Frankfort, 1781), "Concilium," art. 1, nn. 27-29. Certainly he says that titular bishops should be called to a council, but the reason he gives is that although these bishops have no jurisdiction in the diocese assigned to them, they do have jurisdiction by law: "Although the churches of which these bishops are titulars by ordination and consecration are now occupied by unbelieving tyrants, and therefore they have no jurisdiction *in actu secundo* because they have no territory in which to

and more recently F. X. Wernz, J. B. Sägmüller, R. Scherer, J. Laurentius and J. B. Haring.[15] Certain commentators propose the same theory to justify the discipline contained in the Code. N. Jung, for example, writes: "In order to ensure the ecumenicity of the council, all these dignitaries of the Church in our time should be invited, either personally or by a general edict promulgated by the sovereign pontiff, even though it is the residential bishops, whether bishops or archbishops, primates or patriarchs, who alone have a right to be called independent of positive legislation, since they exercise proper, ordinary and real jurisdiction over a given territory. They are in fact the successors of the apostles and, together with the pope, form the Church governing and teaching." [16] A. Vermeersch-

---

govern any subjects . . . nevertheless they do possess jurisdiction *in actu primo* over their titular churches." According to Ferraris, then, the basis for their right to take part in a council is the jurisdiction they possess by law in the dioceses of which they are titulars, and not their episcopal consecration.

[15] F. X. Wernz, *Ius Decretalium*, Vol. II (Rome, 1899), n. 846, p. 1071: "But since titular bishops have no jurisdiction . . . and the business of ecumenical councils is carried out by the power of *jurisdiction* and not that of *orders*, they do *not have* to be called to ecumenical councils. However, they *may* fittingly be called. . . ." Of the same opinion are J. B. Sägmüller, *Lehrbuch des katholischen Kirchenrechts*, Vol. I (Fribourg e. B., 1900), n. 105, p. 391; R. Scherer, *Handbuch des Kirchenrechtes*, Vol. I (Graz, 1886), n. 96, p. 663 and note 11; Ph. de Angelis, *Praelectiones iuris canonici*, Vol. I (Paris, 1877), pp. 260-61. The last specifies that titular bishops who are vicars apostolic must, in his opinion, be called to a council, since they have the episcopal character and they fulfill the same function as residential bishops. See also J. Laurentius, *Institutiones iuris ecclesiastici* (Fribourg e. B., 1914), n. 284, p. 209; J. B. Haring, *Grundzüge des katholischen Kirchenrechtes* (Graz, 1916), n. 100, p. 306.

[16] N. Jung, "Conciles oecuméniques," in *D.D.C.*, Vol. III, cols. 1287-1288.

J. Creusen and K. Mörsdorf are of the same opinion.[17]

Certain authors writing before the present Code, however, were of the opinion that if titular bishops are invited to a council, they necessarily had the right to take part in the decisions, since their being called to the council by the pope entailed a granting of jurisdiction over all the faithful in general. Such is the doctrine of D. Jacobazzi, A. J. Andreucci, Ph. de Angelis and more recently, S. Aichmer; [18] apparently, such is also the doctrine contained in the Code.

According to another doctrine, on the other hand—the one just affirmed by the Decree *Christus Dominus*—all (and only) consecrated bishops, whether diocesan or simply titular, must by right be called to an ecumenical council. R. Bellarmine seems to admit this theory since, without making any distinction, he affirms the right of every bishop (except if excommunicated) to take part in a

---

[17] A. Vermeersch and J. Creusen, *Epitome iuris canonici*, Vol. I, revised ed. by E. Bergh and J. Greco (Malines, 1963), n. 343, p. 323; K. Mörsdorf, *Lehrbuch des Kirchenrechts*, Vol. I (Munich-Paderborn-Vienna, 1964), p. 353.

[18] Cardinal Jacobazzi, *op. cit.*, n. 72, thought that all bishops actually called to a council by the pope receive jurisdiction over all the faithful, "because the bishops actually present in the council, if called, receive jurisdiction over all in general from the pope, and not by reason of some particular church". A. J. Andreucci, *op cit.*, n. 118, agrees: "Because in a case in which titular bishops are called to councils by the pope, they are present as true bishops in orders and dignity, and therefore they are present as governing all the Christian faithful, whom the pope entrusts to them as well as to their fellow bishops gathered together with them, as Jacobazzi teaches. . . ." Ph. de Angelis, *op cit.*, Vol. I, p. 261, agrees with Andreucci. S. Aichner, *Compendium iuris ecclesiastici* (Brescia, 1900), n. 130, p. 458, defends the same doctrine and says that titular bishops who are actually called to a council have the right to vote by divine law.

council.[19] P. Fagnan and P. Laymann are of the same opinion.[20] E. Gonzalez Tellez says explicitly that titular bishops are truly bishops and therefore must be called to a council.[21] This doctrine found its most ardent defender in the Jesuit Jean Vincent Bolgeni. In his work on the episcopate, he teaches that we must distinguish between the particular jurisdiction which bishops exercise in the diocese entrusted to them and the universal jurisdiction which they have over the entire Church because, by being united in the college of bishops, they are in union with the head of the college and under his authority. All consecrated bishops, if they are in union with the other bishops, are invested with this universal jurisdiction, which they possess in virtue of the episcopal consecration itself and which they exercise in an ecumenical council in which they have a right to take part.[22] Bolgeni's doctrine was

---

[19] R. Bellarmine, *De Controversiis christianae fidei,* Vol. II (Cologne, 1619), Book I, "De Concilio et Ecclesia," Ch. 15 (in the edition cited), cols. 27-30, and Ch. 17, col. 34: "...so that no bishop be excluded, wherever he comes from, as long as he is a bishop and is not excommunicated."

[20] P. Fagnan, *Commentaria in quinque Libros Decretalium* (Venice, 1764), Book I, Ch. 1, n. 8, fol. 3; P. Laymann, *Theologia moralis* (Padua, 1733), Book I, Treatise IV, n. 10, p. 48, in the edition cited.

[21] E. Gonzalez Tellez, *Commentaria perpetua in singulos textus quinque librorum Decretalium Gregorii IX* (Lyons, 1715), Book I, Tit. 13, n. 7; in the edition cited, Vol. 1, fol. 443.

[22] G. V. Bolgeni, *L'Episcopato ossia della potestà di governar la Chiesa,* Vol. I (1789), Ch. VII, n. 95, pp. 193-94: "When one considers the entire body of the bishops, whether lawfully gathered in a general council or scattered throughout the Church, then the decisions made by this body regarding the faith are infallible decisions and the laws of discipline place an obligation on the entire Church. Each bishop in the act and by right of his ordination becomes a member of the episcopal body. Consequently he has the right to govern and

rejected by some but accepted by others, such as J. F. Schulte and P. Hinschius.[23]

As we have said, the first doctrine was clearly accepted by the Code of Canon Law, whereas the second theory has been ratified by Vatican Council II. According to the Council, the power of orders and the powers of magisterium and jurisdiction are clearly joined and are rooted in the episcopal consecration itself. It is by this consecration that bishops are members of the episcopal college, and thus it is in virtue of this consecration that they are by right members of an ecumenical council, where the college solemnly exercises its power of magisterium and its power of jurisdiction—its *jurisdictio universalis*.[24]

---

teach the entire Church when he is united with the other bishops and forms the body with them. This is what I call universal jurisdiction in each bishop, which is distinguished from the particular jurisdiction over the dioceses and the assigned people. . . . Therefore universal jurisdiction is to be attributed to the episcopal character alone, and can exist apart from particular jurisdiction over a determined people."

[23] The doctrine of G. V. Bolgeni is disputed especially by F. X. Wernz, *op. cit.*, Vol. II, n. 846, p. 1071. On the other hand it is accepted by J. F. Schulte and P. Hinschius. Cf. J. F. Schulte, *System des allgemeinen katholischen Kirchenrects,* Vol. II (Giessen, 1856), n. 29, pp. 212-13; n. 66, p. 343: "All those have an unconditional right to participate who are necessary members of the hierarchy: the *bishops gathered together* without any consideration of their special hierarchical position or whether or not they may have a diocese"; P. Hinschius, *System des katholischen Kirchenrechts,* Vol. III (Berlin, 1883), n. 179, p. 605: "Meanwhile, from the beginning of the development of the Church, the foundation of the voting qualification of the bishops has not been the fact of their having a diocese, but rather the apostolic character of their position. The titular bishop does not have any less of an apostolic character than the diocesan bishop. . . ."

[24] Cf. Vatican Council II, Dogmatic Constitution *Lumen gentium,* nn. 21-22: *A.A.S.* 57 (1965), pp. 24-27.

Since an ecumenical council is by definition an assembly in which the college of bishops exercises its collegial power, only consecrated bishops are members by right. However, there are others—bishops elected but not yet consecrated, cardinals not yet consecrated bishops, abbots and prelates *nullius,* superior generals of religious orders and of exempt congregations of priests—who may be called, but this is so only in virtue of a regulation of positive Church law, of a privilege granted by the sovereign pontiff. This is the doctrine commonly taught by the theologians and canonists mentioned above.[25] The Decree *Christus Dominus* did not affirm this conclusion, and indeed it should not since it is concerned only with the pastoral office of bishops. Nevertheless, this conclusion may be drawn from the principle established by both the Constitution *Lumen gentium* and the Decree *Christus Dominus.* Both documents make it clear that all (and only) consecrated bishops are by right members of an ecumenical council, where the college of bishops solemnly exercises the full and supreme power that it possesses in the Church of Christ.

(b) This full and supreme power proper to the college of bishops can also be exercised by the bishops not gathered in ecumenical assembly but scattered throughout the world. They exercise it by every act of magisterium or jurisdiction which ap-

[25] According to Suarez, *op. cit.,* Disp. XI, Sect. 1, n. 18 (in *Opera Omnia,* Vol. XII, p. 327), their right to be present at a council is based on customary law. For others, their right is based on pontifical privilege: thus J. B. Sägmüller, *op. cit.,* Vol. I, n. 105, p. 391; R. Scherer, *op. cit.,* Vol. I, n. 96, p. 663. According to others, finally, it is based on both customary law and privilege: P. Laymann, *op. cit.,* n. 10, p. 49; F. Schmalzgrueber, *op. cit., Dissertatio prooemialis,* n. 325: in the edition cited, Vol. I, p. 132; Ph. de Angelis, *op. cit.,* Vol. I, p. 263; F. X. Wernz, *op. cit.,* Vol. II, n. 846, pp. 1071-72; J. B. Haring, *op. cit.,* n. 100, p. 306.

pears as an act of the college itself. In fact there is nothing to prevent the sovereign pontiff—before proposing or defining a point of doctrine, as well as before decreeing some general disciplinary measure concerning the universal Church—from asking, either verbally or in writing, for the adherence or agreement of the bishops scattered throughout the world. Likewise there is nothing to prevent him from approving or accepting a doctrine which the majority of the bishops scattered throughout the world request him to propose or define, just as there is nothing to prevent him from confirming and agreeing to promulgate a law which the majority of the bishops consider necessary and propose to be introduced into the universal Church. In these cases, there is a direct action of the college of bishops, provided the approval or acceptance by the sovereign pontiff includes the will to make this act of magisterium or legislation a true collegial act.[26]

2. *The Council or Synod of Bishops*

The council or synod of bishops was created by Pope Paul VI in his Motu Proprio *Apostolica sollicitudo,* dated September 15, 1965.[27] In an allocution addressed to the members of the Roman curia on September 21, 1963, the pope, responding to the desire expressed by certain Council fathers, had already declared his intention to establish such a synod if the Council so wished.[28] He confirmed this

[26] Cf. Vatican Council II, Dogmatic Constitution *Lumen gentium,* n. 22: *A.A.S.* 57 (1965), pp. 26-27. See W. Onclin, "Collegiality and the Individual Bishop," in *Concilium*, Vol. 8 (New York: Paulist Press, 1965), p. 82.

[27] Pope Paul VI, Motu Proprio *Apostolica sollicitudo,* setting up a synod of bishops for the universal Church, September 15, 1965: *A.A.S.* 57 (1965), pp. 775-80.

[28] Pope Paul VI, Allocution to the officials of the Roman curia, September 21, 1963: *A.A.S.* 55 (1963), pp. 793-800.

intention in an allocution to the Council fathers on September 29, 1963.[29] Then, on November 4, 1964, the Council fathers expressed their will by approving (1,912 votes to 81) the text contained in n. 5 of the schema of the Decree *Christus Dominus*—a text calling for the erection of a synod in which bishops chosen from different parts of the world would render more effective assistance to the supreme pastor of the Church.

Since this council or synod of bishops was established before the final vote on the Decree *Christus Dominus,* the text of n. 5 of the Decree was revised again. In the new text, the Council notes the establishment of the synod of bishops, ratifies it and emphasizes its significance in terms referring to the Motu Proprio *Apostolica sollicitudo.*

Since it is intended to render effective assistance to the supreme pastor in the government of the Church, this synod is not strictly speaking an organ of the college of bishops, capable of performing acts of a collegial nature in the name of the college. Rather it is an organ of the power exercised by the sovereign pontiff, by whom it is called to assist in carrying out the task which belongs to him as the head of the college. Nevertheless, this synod, composed of bishops chosen from all over the world, is an unmistakable sign of the solicitude which all the bishops have regarding the entire Church and of the responsibility they bear toward the universal Church.[30]

---

[29] Pope Paul VI, Allocution to the Council fathers at the beginning of the second session of Vatican Council II, September 29, 1963: *A.A.S.* 55 (1963), pp. 841-59.

[30] According to the Motu Proprio *Apostolica sollicitudo* itself, this synod of bishops is constituted in such a way that it is "(a) a central ecclesiastical institute; (b) acting in the name of the entire universal episcopacy": *A.A.S.* 57 (1965), p. 776.

3. *The Responsibility of the Bishops concerning All the Churches*

The responsibility which the bishops bear concerning the universal Church entails a real solicitude for all the Churches which comprise it. The Decree declares this solemnly in n. 6: "As the legitimate successors of the apostles and members of the episcopal college, bishops should realize that they are always bound together and so should show themselves to be concerned for all the Churches." [31] Because the bishops share the solicitude for the entire Church and for all the churches that comprise it, they should be especially concerned about the regions of the world where the Word of God has not yet been proclaimed, and about the Churches which are in need, especially those in which, because of a lack of priests, the faithful are in danger of straying from the practice of the Christian life and even of losing the faith.

From such principles, the Decree draws some general conclusions. The bishops should make every effort to promote the works of evangelization and of the apostolate and to obtain the support of the faithful for these works. They should see to the proper training of the sacred ministers, as well as the religious and lay helpers, who are to be assigned to work in the missions or in dioceses which are short of clergy. They should even send some of their priests to the missions and dioceses suffering great difficulties if the priests themselves are willing to exercise the sacred ministry there. Finally, they should be conscious of the fact that the particular Church placed in their charge is one with the universal Church, and therefore that the property be-

[31] This aspect of the responsibility of the bishops is based on the encyclical of Pius XII, *Fidei donum*, April 21, 1957: *A.A.S.* 49 (1957), pp. 237ff.

longing to this particular Church is intended to be used also to alleviate the needs of other Churches, especially those which suffer from want or are struck with some calamity.

4. *Active Charity toward Persecuted Bishops*

Since they belong to the universal body of bishops, the bishops also have duties toward the members of that body, and especially those undergoing great suffering. The Decree also reminds the bishops that they should be particularly concerned about "those bishops who are victims of calumnies and persecutions for the name of Christ, those who are in prison or forbidden to exercise their ministry".

II. Bishops and the Apostolic See

Since the first chapter of the Decree deals with the office of the bishops in the Church of Christ, it must necessarily give some consideration to the relationships between each bishop and the apostolic see at Rome. In fact, it is the hierarchical communion of all the bishops with the successor of Peter which brings about the unity of the Church. Given this as a basis, the second part of this chapter defines the power of the bishops in their own dioceses, and then follows with a discussion of the congregations of the Roman curia and their members and officials.

1. *The Bishops' Power in Their Own Dioceses*

(a) In n. 8, the Decree expresses first of all a general principle of the highest importance concerning the relationships between the bishops and the apostolic see. As the successors of the apostles, the bishops, who are the direct pastors of the dioceses which are entrusted to them and which they govern under the authority of the supreme pontiff but in their own name, have *per se* all the ordinary, proper and immediate power necessary for the exercise of their pastoral duties. However, exception is made always and in all matters for the power which the Roman pontiff has, in virtue of his office, to reserve cases to himself or to some other authority.

This statement is absolute and unmistakable. In their own dioceses the bishops have *legislative power*, the power to enact laws of general import for the common good of the diocese. Naturally, they only have the power to pass laws which are not contrary either to the common law of the Church or to the law of the patriarchate, ecclesiastical region or ecclesiastical province. But they may pass laws *praeter ius commune* ("beyond common law") and *praeter ius provinciale et regionale* ("beyond provincial and regional law") concerning all ecclesiastical matters, unless certain matters have been expressly removed from their legislative competence by the supreme authority and are reserved to the supreme authority itself, the pope, or the college of bishops, or to some other authority such as a patriarchal synod, a provincial or national council, or a conference of bishops. The bishops also have *administrative power*, the power to perform all acts of a particular or individual nature, such as nominations to ecclesiastical offices, erection of such offices, granting of privileges and permissions, etc. They may perform all administrative actions necessary or useful for the administration of their dioceses, except those which the supreme authority reserves to itself or to some other ecclesiastical authority. Finally, the bishops have *judiciary power*. In their own dioceses they are the ordinary judges in the first instance, in the external forum, for all ecclesiastical cases, whether personal or real, which are not expressly reserved to a superior judge by the supreme authority.

Is this statement of n. 8 of the Decree something new, and does it constitute a reversal of the law accepted up to now in the Church? It is new in its clearness and generality, and especially in what concerns administrative power. It is not new in what concerns the legislative competence and the judiciary power of the bishops.

Strictly speaking, it is not new in what concerns the legislative, judiciary and coercive power of the bishops. In fact Canon 334, § 1 of the Code states that bishops are the ordinary and immediate pastors of the dioceses entrusted to them; moreover, Canon 335, § 1, declares that bishops have the right to govern their dioceses in spiritual and temporal matters with legislative, judiciary and coercive power which is to be exercised according to the regulations of the holy canons. Therefore it would be wrong to say that, according to the Code, the bishops had the right to pass laws and to judge only in those cases expressly granted to them by common law. According to the Code, bishops have the power to pass laws for their own dioceses provided these laws are not contrary to the provisions of universal Church law or to the law of the province or region containing the diocese, and provided certain matters have not been removed from their legislative competence. According to the Code, then, they have the power to pass laws in all matters which are not reserved to some other authority, but they only have the power to pass laws *praeter ius commune* and *praeter ius provinciale et regionale*. Since dioceses are part of the universal Church, the legislation common to the whole Church applies to the various particular Churches which comprise it. Therefore the bishops, who are legislators in their dioceses, are not competent to enact laws contrary to the common law or to the law of their province or ecclesiastical region. The Sacred Congregation of the Council expressed this view on February 19, 1921, when it declared that the legislative power of the bishops is limited to matters not at all or at least not entirely determined or sanctioned by common law, so that the bishops have no right to make provisions which are contrary to the letter or the spirit of the common law.[32] Along the same line, the Apostolic Signature declared on December 15, 1923, that the legislative power of bishops is limited by the universal laws of the Church and by the particular decrees of the popes.[33] According to the Code, the bishops in principle also have judiciary power—that is, the power to judge in the first instance all ecclesiastical cases which are not expressly reserved by law to a superior judge (Can. 1572, n. 1). Finally, the Code also declares that the bishops have the power of coercion. They see to the execution of the penalties which common law inflicts or orders to be inflicted. They also have the power to enact penalties in order to provide sanctions for diocesan laws, as well as the power to impose penalties by personally pronouncing sentence against a particular offender, according to the rules of law (Cans. 2214, 2220, § 1, 2320). From all of this we may conclude that the statement in n. 8 is not new but simply confirms, in clear and absolute terms, the law already in effect.

The Decree does say something new, however,

---

[32] Cf. *A.A.S.* 13 (1921), p. 228.
[33] Cf. *A.A.S.* 16 (1924), p. 107.

regarding the *administrative competence* of bishops. This competence concerns all those activities not included in the powers spoken of above—that is, all actions of a particular or individual nature which are necessary or useful for the governing of the diocese. Such would be appointments and changes of personnel, erection of ecclesiastical offices, administration of ecclesiastical property or the supervision of the management of such property, all actions pertaining to the safeguarding and supervision of Christian life, etc. The Code of Canon Law makes no mention of administrative power. Naturally, it contains regulations concerning several actions of an administrative nature, and it grants the bishops the competence to perform a certain number of such actions. But according to the Code, the bishops have power to perform only those administrative actions for which they have been expressly granted competence by the Code or by later laws,[34] or perhaps by special acts granting them delegated faculties. The Decree *Christus Dominus,* in n. 8, introduces a new rule which constitutes a reversal of the norm in force up to this time. This new regulation acknowledges that the bishops have all the powers—and therefore the administrative competences—required for the exercise of their pastoral

---

[34] The Code attributes to the bishops the competence to perform actions pertaining to such things as the admission of members of the clergy by incardination or ordination (Cans. 111, 955ff.), the erection or suppression of offices and benefices (Cans. 152, 366, 403, 1414, n. 2), the erection and supervision of confraternities and other ecclesiastical associations of the faithful (Cans. 686ff), the administration of ecclesiastical property (Cans. 1519ff., 1545), etc. Among the canon laws granting wider administrative powers to diocesan bishops, we should note especially the Motu Proprio of Paul VI, *Pastorale munus*, November 30, 1963: *A.A.S.* 56 (1964), pp. 5-12.

office, except those expressly reserved to the supreme pontiff or to some other authority.

The rule thus established is a general one. The bishops have all powers necessary to fulfill their pastoral duties in their dioceses, except those which the supreme authority—that is, the sovereign pontiff or the episcopal college—reserves to itself or attributes to another authority. This rule is perfectly logical. The bishops are the principal pastors in the dioceses entrusted to them and therefore they must have in principle all the powers necessary to accomplish their task. It goes without saying that the powers thus attributed to diocesan bishops are the only powers demanded by the government of their dioceses. The powers pertaining to the government of the universal Church are by their very nature reserved to the sovereign pontiff and the college of bishops. Besides, since the bishops govern their dioceses under the authority of the organs of supreme power, the latter have the right to reserve the regulating of certain matters concerning the government of dioceses either to themselves or to other authorities such as particular councils, episcopal conferences, or, in the Eastern Churches, the patriarch or patriarchal synods.

(b) The general rule set forth in n. 8 led to a more particular rule concerning certain administrative actions—namely, the granting of dispensations from the universal laws of the Church. Since laws are enacted in view of *general* circumstances or conditions, dispensations are sometimes needed and can even be absolutely necessary. In order for bishops to fulfill properly the mission entrusted to them, the Council thought it useful to grant them the power to dispense in particular cases from all universal laws of the Church whenever the spiritual welfare of the faithful requires it, unless special provision was made by the supreme authority.

According to the Code, the bishops could dispense only from those universal laws for which they had been expressly granted power. The Code itself granted diocesan bishops, as well as all ordinaries, this power to dispense from certain universal laws, at least under certain conditions.[35] The Motu Proprio *Pastorale munus* granted them the power to dispense from certain other laws.[36] Other powers of dispensing were granted them by faculties delegated by special acts of the Holy See. Besides these powers, whether ordinary or delegated, concerning certain determined laws, the Code also granted diocesan bishops, as well as other ordinaries, a general power to dispense. According to Canon 81, they have the power to grant dispensations which the apostolic see customarily grants, in a case in which recourse to the Holy See is difficult,[37] what-

[35] Thus the Code confers on diocesan bishops, as on all local ordinaries, the power to dispense: (a) from the law forbidding one to celebrate more than one Mass on the same day (Can. 806, n. 2); (b) from most of the laws forbidding ordination because of irregularities arising from a delict, if the latter be occult (Can. 990, n. 1); (c) from the law concerning the banns of marriage (Can. 1028); (d) from laws regarding the canonical form of marriage and most of the laws containing ecclesiastical impediments to marriage, when there is danger of death (Can. 1043), as well as from laws concerning the same impediments when certain definite extraordinary conditions are fulfilled (Can. 1045, n. 1); (e) from the law forbidding the granting of the nuptial blessing during the closed period (Can. 1108, n. 3); (f) from the law concerning the observance of feast days, as also from the law regarding fast and abstinence (Can. 1245, nn. 1 and 2).

[36] Motu Proprio *Pastorale munus,* especially nn. 2-10, 15-17, 19, 20, 23, 26, 31, 35.

[37] According to the interpretation given by the Commission for the Interpretation of the Code on June 26, 1947

ever may be the cause of the difficulty, and in which any delay in granting the dispensation would very likely cause grave inconvenience. According to Canon 15, they may also grant all dispensations customarily granted by the Holy See in cases where it is doubtful whether the law applies as a result of a doubt concerning a doubt of fact—that is, in case of a *dubium facti*.

At present, according to the Decree *Christus Dominus,* diocesan bishops in principle have the power to grant all dispensations from universal laws in particular cases if they consider the dispensation to be useful for the spiritual welfare of the faithful. This is the general rule, but there are exceptions. The bishops cannot grant dispensations which the supreme authority of the Church reserves to itself or to some other authority.

These provisions concerning the power of diocesan bishops were to go into effect on June 29, 1966. The *vacatio legis* of eight months provided by the Decree was certainly necessary. The Holy See needed the time to draw up a list of matters which it deemed wise, considering the welfare of all, to reserve to its competence alone, and also a list of dispensations which it thought necessary to reserve to itself. This period also allowed it to draw up a list of matters which the Council or the sovereign pontiff wanted to reserve to other constituted authori-

---

(*A.A.S.* 39 [1947], p. 374), in order for the recourse to the Holy See to be difficult, it must be impossible for the ordinary to have recourse to the Holy See through the nuncio or through the apostolic delegate. However the ordinary could grant the dispensations even if the nuncio or the apostolic delegate has faculties to grant the dispensations. Cf. R. Naz, *Traité de droit canonique* (Paris, 1954), Vol. I, n. 316, p. 224; C. Sartori and B. I. Belluco, *Enchiridion canonum seu Sedis Sanctae Responsiones post editum Codicem I.C. datae* (Rome, 1961), on Can. 81, pp. 13-14.

ties, such as the patriarch or patriarchal synod, particular councils or conferences of bishops.

2. The Congregations of the Roman Curia

In n. 9, the Decree deals with the congregations of the Roman curia, those ministries or departments in the service of the Roman pontiff which, in his name and by his authority, exercise the competence (chiefly administrative) assigned to them for the good of both the universal Church and the particular Churches and for the service of pastors. In his allocution to the members of the Roman curia on September 21, 1963, Pope Paul VI announced a reform of the curia.[38] He spoke of this again at the promulgation of the present Decree, making reference to the Decree itself.[39] In fact, in the Decree, the Council fathers expressed the wish that this reform be carried out in accord with the needs of the times and of the various regions and rites, and that it deal with the number of congregations, their name, competence, methods of procedure, and the coordination of their work. They also expressed the wish that the functions of papal legates be more clearly defined, taking into account the pastoral office proper to the bishops.

In n. 10, the Decree discusses the members and officials of these congregations. The congregations are the instruments of central power in the Church; they are at the service of the universal Church and of each of the particular Churches that comprise it. Therefore, it is important that their composition reflect the universal nature of the Church. That is why the Council fathers expressed the wish that, as far as possible, the members of these congregations,

---

[38] Cf. *A.A.S.* 55 (1963), pp. 793-800.

[39] Cf. *A.A.S.* 57 (1965), pp. 978-84, especially pp. 980-81.

as well as their officials and consultors, be selected from different regions of the Church. They also wanted bishops, especially diocesan bishops, to be included among the members of the congregations, since they would be better able to furnish information regarding the mentality, desires and needs of the various churches. Finally, the Council fathers thought it would be useful for the congregations to extend a wider role in their work to lay people known for their special qualities, their knowledge and their experience. The faithful constitute the Church, and it is only fair that the Church, which is theirs and to which they belong as living members, grant them the part which belongs to them in the affairs of the Church.

Study-Club Questions

1. How can the entire mission of the bishops of the Church be called a pastoral mission?

2. Bishops are members of the college of bishops in virtue of the episcopal consecration itself and not in virtue of their assignment to particular Churches. Explain.

3. This Decree should be read in conjunction with the Dogmatic Constitution *Lumen gentium*. What does *Lumen gentium* tell us about the role of bishops in the Church?

4. Mention three major conclusions that this Decree draws from *Lumen gentium*.

5. Do all bishops have a right to take part in an ecumenical council? Explain.

6. What is the difference between a residential bishop and a titular bishop?

7. Can the synod of bishops perform acts of a collegial nature in the name of the college of bishops? Explain.

8. Mention three examples of each of the following powers of diocesan bishops: (1) legislative power; (2) administrative power; (3) judiciary power.

9. Do bishops have a right to enact laws which are contrary to the letter or the spirit of the common law of the Church? Explain.

10. Is n. 8 of this Decree something new, or does it constitute a reversal of the law accepted up to now in the Church? Explain.

11. How does this Decree update the reform of the congregations of the Roman curia?

12. What do the first two words of this Decree proclaim about the missionary activity of the bishops of the Church?

13. How does the bishops' work of teaching, sanctifying and ruling continue Christ's work of redemption and salvation?

14. Does this Decree give bishops the power to grant all dispensations from universal laws in particular cases? Explain.

15. Why should bishops have the power of coercion? How extensive is this power?

16. Does the college of bishops possess full and supreme power in the Church? Explain.

17. Why should diocesan bishops be concerned with the welfare of the universal Church?

18. Is the supreme power of the college of bishops exercised only in an ecumenical council? Explain.

19. Suggest three areas in your diocese where your bishop could promote further apostolic renewal.

20. Mention three important qualities of a good diocesan bishop.

Chapter II

Bishops and Particular Churches or Dioceses

Chapter II of the Decree deals with the mission which bishops have to fulfill in the particular Churches or dioceses entrusted in a special way to their care.

The chapter has three parts. The first, entitled "Diocesan Bishops", considers the diocesan bishops themselves and the pastoral duties which they have to fulfill in the particular Churches assigned to them. The second part is concerned more with the particular Churches themselves and establishes certain norms regarding the division of dioceses. The third and last part is devoted to those who cooperate with diocesan bishops in the fulfillment of their pastoral duties.

I. Diocesan Bishops

The first part, which contains certain prescriptions drawn in large measure from the schema "On the Care of Souls", is concerned with the mission of the bishops in their dioceses.

Since diocesan bishops are by definition the ones assigned to dioceses, this statement begins with an excellent definition of a diocese. A *diocese,* it says, is a portion of the People of God to whom a bishop is assigned as the proper pastor. Thus it is not first of all a territory but a people, and by this word the Decree recalls the magnificent second chapter of the Dogmatic Constitution *Lumen gentium* on the People of God. And because a diocese is above all the People of God, the bishop assigned to it as pastor is no longer to be called residential—a term that puts the emphasis on territory—but diocesan. Certainly the group of the faithful who constitute a diocese will most often be determined by the territory in which they live. However, they may also be determined by other factors, such as the nationality or language or rite of the people who make it up. Thus the diocese is an ensemble of persons, a people, in whom the Church of Christ is present, living and acting. In the diocese, God's people are entrusted to a bishop who is their pastor and who with the aid of his *presbyterium* (all the priests considered as a group) carries out his pastoral duties. Here we have a direct confirmation of the pastoral nature of the episcopal office. And the bishop is not appointed without being immediately associated with his presbyterium. This picture of the diocese is completed with one final brushstroke: the full union of the people with their pastor and their being gathered together in the Holy Spirit through the Gospel and the eucharist.[1]

The *diocesan bishop*, then, is the one who is assigned to a particular Church as its proper, ordinary and immediate pastor, and who, in the name of the Lord himself, although under the authority of the sovereign pontiff, fulfills the threefold episcopal function of teaching, sanctifying and ruling the

[1] Cf. P. Veuillot, "Introduction au décret sur la charge pastorale des évêques dans l'Eglise," in *Documents conciliares* 2 (Paris: Editions du Centurion, 1965), p. 23.

faithful who constitute this particular Church. The text of n. 11 states: "Individual bishops, to whom the care of a particular Church has been committed subject to the authority of the pope, as the proper, ordinary and immediate pastors of their people, feed their sheep in the name of the Lord by exercising the office of teaching, sanctifying and governing in their regard." Thus as a result of this *commissio* by which he is assigned to a diocese, the bishop is directed to exercise toward the people assigned to him the episcopal powers which his episcopal consecration conferred on him. This *commissio,* or act of assigning a diocese to a bishop, is not intended, therefore, to confer on him the episcopal powers of teaching, sanctifying and governing, but to assign to him that portion of the People of God for whom he is to exercise these powers as their proper, ordinary and immediate pastor. By thus being assigned to a particular group of the faithful, he can exercise more effectively the episcopal powers inherent in the episcopate and received by episcopal consecration.[2]

Thus the bishop is to exercise his powers for the benefit of the faithful of a particular Church assigned to him. However, since the message of Christ is intended for all men, however, the bishop should not only care for those who have received the message and have remained faithful to it, but should extend

---

[2] The introductory explanatory note to the Dogmatic Constitution *Lumen gentium* explains why the word *munera* ("offices") and not the word *potestates* ("powers") was used here. The latter could be taken to mean powers fit to be exercised. But the powers which a bishop possesses by his ordination are not fit to be exercised for a determined people; they are not *ad actum impediti* on condition that a portion of the People of God is assigned to him. Rather his power *becomes* directed to action when subjects are assigned to him, as the same note (n. 2) indicates.

his solicitude to include also those who have not known or received it (and therefore do not yet belong to the Church of Christ) and also to those who have received it but have not remained faithful. In fact the bishop is the witness of Christ before all men, responsible to all for the message of goodness and mercy which Christ brought to the world.

After describing in a general way the pastoral office entrusted to a diocesan bishop, the Decree takes up various aspects of this office. After the example and in the light of Chapter II of the *Constitution on the Church,* it considers (nn. 12-16) the different functions of the episcopal mission, with special reference to the needs of the times.

1. *The Office of Teaching*

The first function inherent in the episcopal office is that of teaching Christian doctrine, which the Council of Trent calls the *praecipuum episcoporum munus* (the most important task of the bishops).[3] The Decree describes briefly the object of this teaching, the method to be followed and the means to be used. Naturally the *object* of this teaching is above all the supernatural end of man and the supernatural means which God has put at man's disposal for reaching this end. This is what the Decree calls the whole mystery of Christ. But this teaching should also show men the true value of the things of this earth, understood in the light of supernatural truths. Therefore the teaching should also be concerned with the various questions about which men's consciences today especially need clarification according to the authorized interpretation

---

[3] Cf. Council of Trent, Session V, Decree *De Reform.,* Ch. 2: Mansi, 33, 30; Session XXIV, Decree *De Reform.,* Ch. 4: Mansi, 33, 159. Cf. also Vatican Council II, Dogmatic Constitution *De Ecclesia,* n. 25: *A.A.S.* 57 (1965), pp. 20ff.

of the message of Christ given by the Church. The *method* to be followed, or the way of presenting the doctrine in keeping with the needs of the times, is considered in n. 13. The bishops should not be satisfied with presenting the principles of Christian doctrine, but should also take care to apply them to the circumstances of our age, especially in answering the questions posed—so anxiously sometimes—by the faithful of today. Since they are the representatives of the Church, our mother, the bishops should show special care for the weak and the poor whom our Lord loved with a special love. And since it is especially important today for the Church to enter into dialogue with the human society in which she lives,[4] it is the duty of the bishops first of all to approach men and promote dialogue with them. This same n. 13 gives a brief treatment of the *means* to be used to make this teaching effective. While the traditional means of preaching and catechetical instruction are always to be given preference, nevertheless the modern ways of spreading the doctrine are not to be neglected.

A special section (n. 14) is devoted to catechetical instruction, which was the object of an entire chapter (Ch. V) in the schema "On the Care of Souls". The preparatory Commission on the Discipline of the Clergy and the Christian People had drawn up a schema "On the Catechetical Institution". The part of this schema dealing with catechetical instruction had already been considerably abridged in the schema "On the Care of Souls". In n. 14, the present Decree repeats only the chief provisions. However, in order to emphasize the importance of catechetical instruction, a special number is devoted to it, containing the purpose of this

[4] Cf. Paul VI, Encyclical *Ecclesiam suam,* August 6, 1964: *A.A.S.* 56 (1964), pp. 644-45.

teaching, the methods proper to it, and its sources, which are sacred scripture, tradition, liturgy, and the magisterium and life of the Church. The bishops are directed to see to it that catechists are properly trained for their task and to do their utmost to restore or establish the adult catechumenate.

2. *The Office of Sanctifying*

The second function which bishops have to fulfill is that of sanctifying. They are in fact invested with the fullness of the priesthood, and it is in dependence on the bishops that the priests, who have been consecrated to be fellow-workers of the episcopal order, and the deacons, who have been ordained in view of the ministry, are to exercise their power. Therefore it is the bishops who are primarily responsible for the sanctification of the faithful entrusted to their care, to whom they must dispense the supernatural means of sanctification, the sacraments, and whom they must teach to participate in the liturgical life of the Church, with the eucharist, the holy sacrifice, at its center. The bishops should also promote holiness of life among the priests, religious and laity, each group according to its vocation, and they should give an example of a holy life. Finally, they should be diligent in using every means to foster vocations to the priesthood and the religious life, especially missionary vocations.

3. *The Office of Governing*

The third function proper to bishops is that of governing the particular church entrusted to them (n 16). To fulfill this duty the bishops should, like Christ himself, be good shepherds who know their flock and whose sheep know them, and they should be true fathers to those in their care. Therefore they should be personally acquainted with their fellow-workers, the priests, and see to it that they are assured of those conditions for their spiritual, intellectual and material life which will make the exercise of their ministry truly effective. They should also be acquainted with their flock. Obviously they cannot know personally all the faithful in their care, but they should strive to become fully acquainted with the needs of their faithful and the conditions in which they live. As good pastors, they will also be concerned about the separated brethren and will be sure to encourage ecumenical activities in the spirit of the Church. Finally, they should show the non-baptized the true charity of Christ, whose witnesses they are before all men.

After treating the various functions of the episcopal office, the Decree deals briefly, in n. 17, with certain aspects of the apostolate. The bishops should foster a close and complete coordination of all the works of the apostolate. Such an action of coordinating all the institutes of the apostolate, under the direction of the bishop, will more clearly manifest the unity of the diocese. The bishops should encourage the faithful to become aware of their duty to engage in the apostolate and to support the works of the apostolate. They should diligently promote and encourage associations in which the faithful either directly or indirectly pursue some supernatural end. The bishops should erect similar associations which, according to the usual terminology, are called ecclesiastical associations. They should give their support to associations which the faithful themselves, acting out of a natural right to form associations, establish with the purpose of pursuing some supernatural end not reserved to the hierarchy alone.[5] Finally, the bish-

[5] Cf. W. Onclin, "Principia generalia de fidelium associa-

ops should take care that the works of the apostolate are adapted to modern needs.

The bishops are directed to show special care for certain groups of the faithful in n. 18, a text which repeats briefly the considerations developed and the regulations proposed in the schema "On the Care of Souls" (Chap. IV, nn. 47-52). In fact, by reason of their professional activity or the particular circumstances of their lives, certain groups of the faithful are deprived of the benefits of parish life and the ordinary apostolate. This is the case with most emigrants, exiles, refugees, sailors, airplane personnel, nomads and many others. The bishops should show a special concern for such persons, as well as for tourists who spend some time in their dioceses, and they should study the pastoral questions regarding these people especially in episcopal conferences.

Then there follows (n. 19) a declaration—no less important for having been introduced quite late into the text—stating that bishops should enjoy freedom and independence of civil authorities. Since bishops are at the service of the Church, a sovereign society in the supernatural order willed by God, they should enjoy that full freedom which is necessary for the fulfillment of their office, and no one may hinder their activity nor forbid them free communication with the apostolic see, with other ecclesiastical authorities or with their subjects.

The freedom and independence necessary for the Church to work toward her spiritual and supernatural goal also includes the exclusive right of the Church to appoint bishops. In n. 20, therefore, it states that the right to appoint and institute

---

tionibus," in *Apollinaris* 36 (1963), pp. 86ff., and in *La Sacra Congregazione del Concilio* (Vatican City, 1964), pp. 499ff.

bishops belongs to the competent ecclesiastical authority and to it alone. The agreements made with civil authorities may limit the exercise of this freedom, but they cannot impair it in principle. The Council expresses the wish, however, that in the future civil authorities should not be granted any right or privilege of election, nomination, presentation or designation with regard to the episcopal office. It also asks those civil authorities to whom such a right has been granted to freely forego it by agreement with the Holy See.

The Decree concludes its remarks on diocesan bishops with a brief statement on the question of the resignation of bishops from office. The question whether or not it was fitting to set a certain age limit for the episcopal office was widely discussed. The text drawn up by the preparatory commission stated explicitly that a diocesan bishop was assumed to be resigning at the age of 75, though the pope would still have to decide whether to accept such a resignation or postpone it. The conciliar commission thought it best not to introduce into the Decree a regulation fixing an age limit. Therefore, nothing was said on this point in the schema "On Bishops and the Government of Dioceses", which was discussed during the second session of the Council. There was only a note stating that any age limit used as a reason leading to resignation should be extended to 75 years complete. The discussion of this schema showed that certain Council fathers were agreeable to the imposition of an age limit, but that a majority were opposed to it because of the respect due to the person of the bishop and even more because of the original significance of the episcopal office. That is why the schema "On the Pastoral Office of Bishops in the Church," presented at the third session, no longer provided for an age limit for the office of diocesan bishops. Rather it was satisfied with requesting the bishops to offer their resignation willingly, either on their own initiative or when invited by the competent authority, if because of old age or for some other serious reason they became less capable of carrying out their office. This is the text contained in n. 21 of the Decree.

However, the Motu Proprio *Ecclesiae sanctae* of August 6, 1966, in laying down the measures for carrying out the provisions of the Decree *Christus Dominus*, gave more details regarding the Council's request to the diocesan bishops. It urgently asks them to offer their resignation to the competent authority when they completed their seventy-fifth year (I, n. 11). This is not a strict obligation, but an urgent request. It does not ask the bishops to resign, but to present their resignation. It would then be up to the competent authority to judge whether, in the particular circumstances, the resignation should be accepted or postponed.

II. Diocesan Boundaries

The question of diocesan boundaries was already treated in the schema "On Bishops and the Government of Dioceses", which devoted Chapter IV to the division of dioceses and ecclesiastical provinces. It seemed logical to separate these two questions and to set forth the principles governing diocesan boundaries in the chapter dealing with the office of bishops in the particular Churches entrusted to them. In fact it is only natural that Chapter II, which is concerned with the office of diocesan bishops, should take up the question of the best ways to determine diocesan boundaries.

It is to this question that the Decree addresses itself (nn. 22-24) in two pages that are compact, clear and fully adapted to present conditions.

The basic *principle* is presented in n. 22. Diocesan boundaries are to be determined in the light of the purpose of the diocese; the portion of the People of God who make up that diocese must reflect the Church of Christ. In order to carry out this purpose effectively, consideration must be given to the distribution of population, the extent of territory and the possibility of the bishop's fulfilling his pastoral duties. The Decree directs that diocesan boundaries be revised and that, depending on the particular needs of the faithful, this be carried out either by dividing dioceses that are too large or combining those which are too small or reorganizing dioceses that cannot be divided. The new internal organization mentioned in the Decree applies to such extensive dioceses as New York, Boston, Paris and Milan. In large cities the Christian life should be directed from a single center, which makes it difficult to erect several dioceses within the territory of a single city. In such cases it is preferable to divide the diocese into several sections, each entrusted to an auxiliary bishop armed with special extensive powers, but always maintaining the basic unity of direction for the territory as a whole.

In n. 23 the Decree sets forth the *rules to be followed* in revising diocesan boundaries: (1) According to the first rule, the various differences among the People of God in a particular diocese should be maintained as far as possible. In principle, then, it is highly desirable for the territory of a diocese to be continuous. (2) The second rule states that the territorial extent of a diocese should be such that the bishop, assisted by others, can personally make pastoral visitations and can direct and coordinate the works of the apostolate. On the other hand, mindful of the needs of the universal Church, it should provide a field of activity extensive enough for the bishop and his priests to be able to work usefully. (3) Finally, according to the third rule, care must be taken that each diocese have at its disposal a sufficient number of competent priests.

This section concludes (n. 24) by noting that the competent episcopal conferences should study the question of the division of dioceses. The first schema provided for a permanent commission of bishops. The Decree enjoins this task on the episcopal conferences themselves, though they may, if they deem it useful, set up a special commission to carry out the study. In any case, it is up to the conferences to draw conclusions and to submit their recommendations to the apostolic see.

III. Assistants of the Diocesan Bishop in the Pastoral Office

The decree mentions the following assistants of the diocesan bishop: (1) coadjutor and auxiliary bishops; (2) members of the diocesan curia and pastoral council; (3) the diocesan clergy, in which pastors and priests in charge of supraparochial or supradiocesan works are dealt with separately; (4) religious, who belong to the diocesan family to the extent that they devote themselves to the apostolate.

The schema "On Bishops and the Government of Dioceses" spoke of coadjutor and auxiliary bishops, but did not mention any other persons assisting the diocesan bishop in the fulfillment of his pastoral office. The schema "On the Care of Souls", however, made some important remarks concerning the duties of pastors (Chap. II, nn. 13-18), as well as the contributions of religious to the apostolate and the relationships between religious and the bishop of the diocese (Chap. III, nn. 19-40). Since many Council fathers remarked that consideration should be given to the diocesan clergy and to the members of the diocesan curia, the Decree deals with all the assistants of the diocesan bishop in a special part of Chapter II.

1. *Coadjutor and Auxiliary Bishops*

(a) *Definition of terms.* The two terms, auxiliary bishop and coadjutor bishop, are spelled out in more detail in the Decree, which makes certain changes in the legislation. These definitions are drawn from the provisions contained in nn. 25 and 26 of the Decree.

Auxiliary bishops are established for the needs of the diocese, and they should be appointed whenever the diocesan bishop cannot accomplish all the episcopal duties by himself, whether because of the extensive territory covered by the diocese, or the great number of inhabitants, or some special conditions of the apostolate. Therefore they are always to be given to the see (*sedi dati*). Further, they are always appointed without right of succession.

The *coadjutor bishop,* on the other hand, is appointed in exceptional cases only, and is to be attached to the person of the diocesan bishop in order to assist him personally in fulfilling his episcopal office. Hence he is always *personae datus,* and is always appointed with the right of succession.[6]

[6] The Code (Can. 350) gives the name coadjutors to

(*b*) *The powers of auxiliary and coadjutor bishops.* The Decree presents in n. 25 a twofold principle regarding the powers with which auxiliary and coadjutor bishops are to be invested. On the one hand the powers which they enjoy must not jeopardize the unity of direction in the diocese. On the other hand they must be provided with the powers necessary for them to fulfill their pastoral work effectively and to assure them the respect due their episcopal dignity.

Unity of government in the diocese demands that auxiliary and coadjutor bishops always carry out their pastoral duties in full harmony with the diocesan bishop (n. 25).

Both the effectiveness of their pastoral activity and the respect due their dignity as bishops require that they be given certain powers in the diocese. This is why the Decree (n. 26) introduces into Canon Law some new prescriptions regarding auxiliary and coadjutor bishops.

Auxiliary bishops should be appointed vicars general or at least episcopal vicars. The diocesan bishop is obliged to confer one of these offices on them. The office of episcopal vicar is also new in the law. As will be explained in detail later, the office of episcopal vicar confers by right on those who hold it the same powers as are granted to vicars general, but only in one part of the diocese, or only for one special kind of diocesan business, or only concerning the faithful of one

---

auxiliary bishops as well as to coadjutor bishops who, according to the Decree, are given to the person of the diocesan bishop. According to the Code we may distinguish three kinds of coadjutors: (a) coadjutors given to the see; (b) coadjutors given to the person of the diocesan bishop with the right of succession; (c) coadjutors given to the person of the bishop without the right of succession, and only these last are called auxiliary bishops (Can. 350, § 3).

particular rite. But if auxiliary bishops are appointed episcopal vicars, they will in no way be dependent on the vicar general or vicars general, but only on the diocesan bishop.

Furthermore, the powers and faculties enjoyed by auxiliary bishops do not expire with the office of the diocesan bishop. When the episcopal see is vacant, therefore, they do not lose the powers which they held by right as vicars general or episcopal vicars.

Finally the Council expressed the wish that, when the episcopal see is vacant, the government of the diocese should be entrusted to the auxiliary bishop, or to one of them if there are several, by those who by law are to provide for this government. During the discussion in the aula of the Council, some of the fathers had suggested that, when the see was vacant, the government of the diocese should be entrusted by right to the auxiliary bishop or to the oldest among several auxiliaries. The Council preferred to maintain the prerogatives of those who, according to the Code, are to appoint an administrator for the interim, but it also expressed to them the wish just mentioned—a wish repeated in the Motu Proprio *Ecclesiae sanctae* (I, n. 13).

The *coadjutor bishop* must be appointed vicar general. The diocesan bishop is obliged to confer this office on him. According to the schema "On Bishops and the Government of Dioceses", the appointing of a coadjutor bishop would *ipso facto* include giving him the power of jurisdiction belonging by right to the vicar general, and this without the diocesan bishop being able to reserve certain matters to himself. During the discussion of this schema at the second session of the Council, this proposal was severely criticized. The appointment of a vicar general *a iure,* not appointed by the bishop of the diocese and therefore in some way independent of him, might jeopardize—were one to insist on it rightly—the unity of government of the diocese. Mindful of this criticism, the conciliar commission changed the statement so that the Decree provides that the coadjutor bishop be appointed vicar general by the diocesan bishop on whom he is to be dependent (like every other vicar general) and who may reserve to himself any matters which he thinks should be handled personally. The Decree adds, however, that in special cases the coadjutor bishop can be granted wider faculties by the competent authority. The section ends by directing the diocesan bishop and the coadjutor to consult together on matters of greater importance.

2. *The Diocesan Curia and Diocesan Councils*

The Decree lays down *general principle* concerning the diocesan curia that it should be organized in such a way that it becomes a suitable instrument in the hands of the bishop not only for administering the diocese but also for carrying out the works of the apostolate. This constitutes a change in the accepted idea of a diocesan curia. According to the Code (Can. 363, § 1), in fact, the diocesan curia consists of people who assist either the bishop or the one taking the bishop's place in administering the diocese. The mind of the Code, then, is that the people who make up the diocesan curia assist the bishop in the government of the diocese by cooperating with administrative duties or by fulfilling judiciary functions. According to the new concept, stated in n. 27 of the Decree, the diocesan curia is called to assist the bishop not only in governing the diocese but also in organizing and carrying out the works of the apostolate. Priests and lay people who belong to it should realize that they are at the service of the entire pastoral ministry of the bishop.

The other *more specific provisions,* also contained in n. 27, concern certain offices of the curia and certain institutions, many of which are new in the law.

The *office of vicar general* remains the most important in the diocesan curia, as the Decree expressly states. The law now in effect concerning this office is in no way changed. In principle, at least when demanded for the effective administration of the diocese, only one vicar general is to be appointed. Where differences of rite or territorial extent demand it, however, several vicars general may be appointed by the bishop (Can. 366, §§ 1 and 3). The vicars general are the assistants of the diocesan bishop. By right they enjoy all the administrative competences which the bishops possess by ordinary law (Can. 368, § 1). They have no judiciary competence, for that is granted to the *officialis,* whom the bishop is obliged to appoint (Can. 1573, § 1).[7] However, by right they enjoy these administrative competences throughout the entire territory, for the jurisdiction of the vicars general cannot be limited territorially (Can 368, § 1). Furthermore, they possess these powers in all matters, except those which the bishop reserves to himself and those which by law demand a special mandate of the bishop (Can. 368, § 1). Thus their administrative competence is ordinary but vicarial, and they are included among the local ordinaries (Can. 198).

[7] Cf. K. Mörsdorf, *Rechtsprechung und Verwaltung im kanonischen Recht* (Freiburg i. Br., 1941), pp. 66-67; E. Eichmann and K. Mörsdorf, *Lehrbuch des Kirchenrechts auf Grund des Codex Iuris Canonici* (Munich-Paderborn-Vienna, 1964) , Vol. I, § 75, pp. 430-31.

They also have the usual faculties granted by the Holy See to the local ordinary, and they may execute rescripts sent to the bishop provided the contrary is not expressly stated and provided the bishop has not been chosen because of his personal qualities (Can. 368, § 2).

According to the Code, vicars general are freely appointed by the bishop, who can also dismiss them if he thinks fit (Can. 366, § 2). The Decree introduces an exception to this rule, stating that the bishop is obliged to make his coadjutor bishop the vicar general, and he is obliged to make the auxiliary bishops either vicars general or episcopal vicars. With this single exception, the Council did not change the law in this matter. It completed it, however, in creating the office of episcopal vicar.

The *office of episcopal vicar* is a new institution in Canon Law; it has been introduced to help the bishop govern and direct his diocese more effectively. In keeping with the needs of the diocese, the bishop may appoint one or several episcopal vicars, just as he may appoint one or several vicars general. The office of episcopal vicar confers by right the same powers granted to vicars general by common law, but only for a particular section of the diocese, or for a special kind of diocesan business, or for the faithful of a particular rite. Thus episcopal vicars are assistants of the bishop, but their power does not necessarily extend throughout the entire territory. Their competence may in fact be limited territorially, but this is not necessarily so. If it extends to the entire territory, it will be limited either to certain matters or to the faithful of a particular rite. However, in the particular domain assigned to them, episcopal vicars have administrative competence, but neither legislative nor judiciary power. Their jurisdiction, like that of the vicars general, is ordinary and vicarial, and thus they are also local ordinaries. In the portion of territory assigned to them, or the particular domain allotted to them, they possess jurisdiction in all matters, except those which the bishop might reserve to himself or those which by law demand a special mandate from the bishop. As the Motu Proprio *Ecclesiae sanctae* states, the bishop is free to reserve certain matters to himself or to the vicar general or, if there are several, to one of the vicars general (I, n. 14). He is also free to give the episcopal vicars or the vicar general alone or the vicars general alone a special mandate required by law for certain matters.

Like the vicars general, the episcopal vicars enjoy, within the limits of their competence, the usual faculties granted to the bishop by the Holy See. Likewise, within the same limits, they have the right to execute rescripts sent to the bishop, provided the contrary is not expressly stated and provided the bishop has not been chosen because of his own personal qualities.[8]

Like the vicars general, the episcopal vicars are freely appointed by the bishop. However, according to *Ecclesiae sanctae*, they may be appointed only for a limited time, to be determined in the

---

[8] In n. 14, the Motu Proprio *Ecclesiae sanctae* applies to an episcopal vicar the same provisions of Canon 44 concerning the granting of rescripts by an ordinary once another ordinary has refused. The Motu Proprio also resolved a controversy. It states that in a case in which a request was refused by a vicar general or an episcopal vicar, it cannot *validly* be granted by another vicar general or episcopal vicar of the same bishop even if the latter knows the reasons for the refusal. The authors disagreed on the answer to his question. Cf. A. van Hove, *De Rescriptis* (Malines, 1936), n. 174, p. 163; J. Kinane, "Can a Vicar-General Grant a Petition Refused by Another Vicar-General?" in *Irish Ecclesiastical Record* 39 (1932), pp. 304-05.

letter of appointment (I, n. 14). Exception is made for auxiliary bishops who, if not made vicars general, must be appointed episcopal vicars, and that without any time limit. Finally, when the episcopal see is vacant, the episcopal vicars who are not auxiliary bishops lose their jurisdiction, as do vicars general. However, the Motu Proprio executing the Decree recommends that the vicar capitular grant them delegated powers in order to ensure proper government for the diocese (I, n. 14).

The *councils commissioned to assist the bishop in directing the diocese* are also considered in the Decree. They should be reorganized to meet present needs. Mentioned in the Decree are the *cathedral chapter,* which is "the Senate and the council" of the bishop (Can. 391, § 1), the *council of consultors,* which fulfills the function of the cathedral chapter if such be lacking (Cans. 423 and 427), and other councils.

This term "other councils" refers first of all to the *priests' senate,* spoken of in the *Decree on the Ministry and Life of Priests (Presbyterorum ordinis).* In order to ensure that the bishop and his priests work closely together, this Decree orders the establishing of "a group or senate of priests". It is to operate in a manner adapted to modern circumstances and needs and have a form and norms to be determined by law. By its counsel this body will be able to give effective assistance to the bishop in his government of the diocese (n. 7). Hence there must be a priests' senate in each diocese, as is also affirmed in the Motu Proprio *Ecclesiae sanctae* (I, n. 15). This senate should represent all the priests working in the diocese, whether secular or religious. It is up to the bishop to decide how the senate is to be set up, but, as the Motu Proprio states, it is advisable for all the bishops of the same territory to come to an agreement on what measures they should adopt on the subject (n. 17).

In setting up these norms, the bishops should see to it that the senate be truly representative of the presbyterium. To make sure that it is so, it seems best that at least part of the members be chosen by the priests themselves.

Like the cathedral chapter, the priests' senate is called the *senate* of the bishop. It is a consultative commission, and therefore is called to assist the bishop with its advice in directing the diocese and carrying out the works of the apostolate. The question arises whether this council is intended to replace the cathedral chapter or the council of consultors and, in case the latter are retained, how the competences of the cathedral chapter and the council of consultors are to be distinguished from that of the priests' senate. The Decree *Presbyterorum ordinis* does not answer this question; it simply says that the law should determine the structure and function of this council of priests. The Motu Proprio *Ecclesiae sanctae* directs the bishops to take the necessary measures to determine the competence proper to each of these councils and to coordinate their activity. It also says that, until the revision of the Code, the cathedral chapter and the council of consultors are to maintain the function and competence granted them by the present law. The Commission on the Revision of the Code of Canon Law will undoubtedly propose more detailed norms on this matter.

Moreover, the Decree *Christus Dominus* also provides for a *pastoral council* which, unlike the priests' senate, is not obligatory. However, it is the wish of the Council that it be set up in each diocese. The pastoral council is not a senate called to assist the bishop in governing the diocese or in actually organizing the works of the apostolate. It has the unique mission of studying and examining questions concerning pastoral action and of formulating the initiatives to be taken and the directions to be followed in order to carry out these works in practice. Unlike the priests' senate, the pastoral council will consist not only of priests and religious but also of specially chosen laymen. Like the priests' senate, it has only a consultative voice. According to the provisions of *Ecclesiae sanctae,* it is up to the bishop to establish the norms by which it is to be set up and to carry out its functions (I, n. 16). However, as in the case of the priests' senate, it is advisable for all the bishops in the same territory, gathered in episcopal conference, to enact similar legislation in this matter (I, n. 17).

3. *The Diocesan Clergy*

The diocesan clergy were not even mentioned in the schema "On Bishops and the Government of Dioceses". Doubtless the reason for this omission was the fact that a special decree on priests was also foreseen. However, they should also be considered in the decree on the office of bishops since they are the priests who are attached to the diocese and devote their whole activity to it, and who are the principal assistants of the bishop. Hence the Decree *Christus Dominus,* which considers the pastoral office of bishops in their dioceses, gives a rather extensive treatment of the role of diocesan priests. The Decree states that they constitute one *presbyterium,* and form one true family, with the bishop as father. In order to make the priests' pastoral activity more fruitful, the Decree recommends that dialogue take place between the bishop and his priests and among the priests themselves. It reminds the priests that, since they are members of one and the same diocesan family, they should feel united among themselves and should help each other spiritually and materially. Finally, the Decree states that it is the task of the bishop to assign them their pastoral duties in the diocese. Since he is the head of the diocesan family, he should direct their pastoral activity, and therefore should be completely free in distributing the various pastoral duties. Hence any rights and privileges restricting this freedom in any way are abolished. Such are the provisions of the Decree concerning diocesan priests in general.

The Motu Proprio *Ecclesiae sanctae* enacts various measures intended to ensure the bishop true freedom in distributing the duties in his diocese. From now on the Holy See no longer reserves to itself the bestowal of benefices and offices, except those which are consistorial. The statutes of the foundations of benefices may no longer contain any clauses restricting the freedom of the bishop in bestowing these benefices. Privileges entailing no obligation which restrict the right of the bishop in bestowing non-consistorial offices and benefices are suppressed. Also suppressed are all rights of nomination, election or presentation of priests for an office or a parochial benefice. However, if these privileges or rights are introduced by a treatise with the Holy See or by a contract with either physical or moral persons, they cannot be suppressed without the agreement of the interested parties. All customs restricting this same freedom of the bishop are likewise abrogated. Finally, the provision of competitive examinations for benefices involving the care of souls is also suppressed (I, n. 18).

Two categories of diocesan priests are singled out for special mention: priests in charge of supraparochial or supradiocesan activities, and pastors.

(a) *Supraparochial diocesan ministers,* who are in charge of either a part of the diocese, or a special category of the faithful, or a particular kind of activity, are unknown as such in Canon Law. The Motu Proprio *Ecclesiae sanctae* (I, n. 19) includes in this category the deans, who are also called rural vicars or archpriests. These are freely appointed by the bishop, but can be designated only for a limited time, to be determined by particular law. The bishop should grant them the powers necessary for them to promote and direct the common pastoral activity in their particular district. The bishop should consult them regarding the appointment, transfer and replacement of pastors living in their district. These provisions are something new in the law. Also new is the mention of priests in charge of supradiocesan work who are especially recommended to the care of the bishop in whose diocese they live.

(b) Naturally the *pastors* are the direct fellow-workers of the bishop since they are in charge of the souls in a particular section of the diocese, the parish, to which they are assigned and which they direct under the authority of the bishop. They exercise their pastoral duties in the name of the bishop for that portion of the People of God entrusted to them. The mission they help to fulfill is the mission of the bishop himself, and in fulfilling it they share in the threefold episcopal office of teaching, sanctifying and governing. The provisions of the Decree on each of these functions repeat what was said concerning the bishops, but adapted to the conditions of the parish ministry. These considerations briefly sum up the ideas developed in the schema "On the Care of Souls" (nn. 13-17). Certain statements of the Decree clearly show its new spirit and deserve to be pointed out. Common life among the priests attached to the same parish is strongly recommended because it promotes apostolic action and offers the faithful an example of charity and unity. Pastors should have a true missionary spirit and therefore extend their solicitude to all those living in the parish. Being shepherds, they should know their flock and work to develop a community spirit. Finally, since the pastors and curates attached to the same parish are at the service of the same community, they should cooperate fully in their common work by helping one another and supporting one another in a fraternal way.

Concerning the appointment, transfer and removal of pastors, the Decree introduces more new regulations. They spring from the principle that the good of souls, which is the *raison d'être* of the pastoral office, demands that the office of pastors be stable but not permanent. The bishop who directs the diocese should enjoy complete freedom in appointing pastors, and should be in a position to provide more easily for the replacing or removing of a pastor. Therefore the Decree abolishes the distinction between movable and immovable pastors and announces that a simpler procedure for transfering and replacing pastors is to be introduced. According to *Ecclesiae sanctae,* until the revised code is promulgated, this procedure will be that provided by the Code for movable pastors (Cans. 2157-2261), at least in the Latin Church (I, n. 20).

Concerning the matter of priests resigning from their office because old age or some other reason has made them less capable of fulfilling their duties, the rule established for bishops is to be applied. The Decree invites them to resign from their office either on their own initiative or at the request of the bishop. The Motu Proprio makes the same provision. Pastors who have reached the age of 75 are requested to hand in their resignation to their bishop, who may accept it or postpone it depending on the circumstances.

Finally, concerning the erection and suppression of parishes and changes in their boundaries, the bishop should act on his own authority in taking those measures which he deems necessary or useful for the good of souls.

4. *Religious*

From the first moment of discussion until the last, this particular part of the Decree was the object of long and sometimes difficult negotiations between the commission on bishops and that on religious. The proposed regulations were then discussed at length in the aula of the Council, and the numerous interventions by the bishops, as well as the many contradictory amendments they proposed, demonstrated the great importance they attached to this question. In their final form the provisions of the Decree are prudent, but they are not always as precise and clear as one might wish.

First a *general principle* is set forth (n. 33). All religious, and also the members of other institutes who profess the evangelical counsels (since, with respect to the rules established in this Decree, they are likened to the religious), have the duty of working for the good of the universal Church and for the good of the particular Churches that comprise it. This duty obliges the religious to devote themselves to the works of the apostolate which are in keeping with the nature of the particular institute to which they belong.

The basic principle is further developed in n. 34. The needs of the apostolate in modern times demand a great participation by religious in the various works of the apostolic ministry. In the exercise of the apostolate, they are the fellow workers of the bishops and are dependent on their authority. Religious priests, first of all, are called to devote themselves to the apostolate. They were ordained for the priestly ministry and for that reason are, like diocesan priests, fellow workers of the episcopal order. Religious laity and women religious, since they consecrate themselves to the Lord, should for that reason be greatly concerned for the spiritual welfare of the diocesan family to which they belong. In our day especially they can be of a great help to the hierarchy.

Specific principles are set forth in n. 35. They determine to what extent the religious, especially those engaged in the apostolate, are dependent on the bishop, and to what extent they are subject to their superiors. Here we can mention only the essential points.

(a) In carrying out the works of the apostolate, religious called to such a task are fellow workers of the bishop, to whom they are subject and whom they should acknowledge and respect as the successor of the apostles. Moreover, religious should be disposed to help willingly in the various pastoral ministries whenever the bishop asks them. Institutes not dedicated to the purely contemplative life may even be called by the bishop to help in pastoral ministries; however, in allotting these ministries, the bishop should take into account the particular nature of each institute.

(b) Religious in the apostolate, however, should remain faithful to the spirit of their institute and to the observance of their rule, and they are dependent on their superiors in all matters pertaining to this. The bishops themselves should see to it that they fulfill their obligations as religious.

(c) Exemption mainly concerns the internal life of the orders and congregations. However, it does not concern this exclusively. It also permits the sovereign pontiff to use religious for the good of the universal Church, and other authorities on whom exempt religious depend (as in the case of the Oriental churches) to use them for the good of the particular Churches under their jurisdiction. Exemption does not, however, infringe upon the jurisdiction the bishops have over all those who carry out pastoral duties in the diocese.

(d) All religious, both exempt and non-exempt, are subject to the jurisdiction of the local ordinaries, as well as to that of particular councils and episcopal conferences in various matters. These matters include: divine worship (but without prejudice to differences of rite); the care of souls; preaching to the people; religious and moral education of the faithful, especially of children (the bishop's task being to direct and supervise this work); catechetical instruction and liturgical formation; the behavior proper to the clerical state. Concerning this last, religious are therefore subject to local regulations in effect regarding ecclesiastical dress and attendance at shows, as well as those forbidding the clergy to belong to certain societies, and other rules (*Ecclesiae sanctae,* I, n. 25). Naturally religious, exempt or non-exempt, are subject to all the particular canonical laws concerning public order.

The most delicate question of all concerns the rights of bishops relative to schools conducted by religious. According to the Decree, the bishops are competent in everything pertaining to the general organization and supervision of Catholic institutions of learning, while the religious take care of the internal direction of the institutions belonging to them. The terms of the Decree are general and do not specify what is included in the general organization of schools that belongs to the competence of the bishops. The Motu Proprio *Ecclesiae sanctae* contains some specifics, but still does not provide the desired clarity. According to I, n, 39, the general organization of institutions of Catholic learning (and therefore also of institutes conducted by religious) includes the distribution of Catholic schools in the diocese and cooperation among them. It also implies whatever supervision is required to make sure that the schools are as capable as other schools in pursuing the cultural and social purposes for which they were established. Thus the local ordinaries have the right to visit the schools either personally or by sending delegates, and also to visit colleges, youth centers, hospitals, orphanges and other institutions founded to perform works of either spiritual or temporal charity, except those internal schools intended only for the students of the religious institutes. However, the Motu Proprio directs the bishops and episcopal conferences to enact measures pertaining to the general organization of schools conducted by religious only after conferring with the major religious superiors about unifying all plans concerning the schools—as called for by the Decree (I, n. 35).

(e) Cooperation between religious institutes and the diocesan clergy is also recommended in general terms in n. 35 of the Decree, which strives to ensure close coordination of all apostolic works and activities. It is up to the Holy See to bring about this coordination in the Church as a whole, to the bishops in their own dioceses, and to patriarchal synods and episcopal conferences in their own territory.

(f) In order to bring about better understanding and cooperation between bishops and religious, the Decree asks (at the end of this chapter) for bishops and religious superiors to meet at set times, and as often as seems fitting, to deal with questions pertaining to the apostolate in their territory.

The Motu Proprio *Ecclesiae sanctae* contains many more provisions pertaining to the relationships between bishops and religious, but it is not necessary to point out all of them in commenting on the text of the Decree.

Study-Club Questions

1. What is this Decree's definition of a diocese? Compare this definition to Chapter II of the Dogmatic Constitution *Lumen gentium* on the People of God.

2. What is a diocesan bishop? To whom must he minister?

3. Why is teaching the most important duty of bishops? How are they to exercise this duty? How does your bishop exercise this duty?

4. What does n. 14 tell us about: (1) the purpose of catechetical instruction; (2) the methods proper to it; (3) its sources?

5. What do we mean when we say that bishops are invested with the "fullness of the priesthood"?

6. To be a good shepherd, a bishop must be acquainted with the needs of his flock. Is your bishop acquainted with your needs and the needs of all other people in your diocese? Explain.

7. What does this Decree mean when it says that bishops should be free and independent of civil authorities?

8. Do laymen have a duty to engage in apostolic work? Explain.

9. What does n. 21 tell us about the resignation of bishops?

10. What is the best way to determine diocesan boundaries? Does your diocese need to revise its boundaries? Explain.

11. What is the difference between an auxiliary bishop and a coadjutor bishop?

12. What are some of the functions of a diocesan curia? Who may belong to a diocesan curia?

13. What is the difference between vicars general and episcopal vicars? What are some of their duties?

14. Mention some of the duties of the following: (1) the cathedral chapter; (2) the council of consultors; (3) the priests' senate; (4) the pastoral council?

15. What does this Decree recommend to make the pastoral activity of diocesan priests more fruitful?

16. What are some of the duties of supraparochial diocesan priests?

17. What are the duties of diocesan pastors?

18. To what extent are diocesan religious subject to the bishop?

19. What are religious institutes? Can you mention the work of three religious institutes in your diocese?

20. To what extent are religious subject to their superiors? Why most a religious be subject to the authority of his superior and to the authority of his bishop?

Chapter III

On Bishops Collaborating for the Common Good of Various Churches

The third chapter of the Decree contains three parts. The first, and certainly the most important, concerns the cooperation of the bishops in serving various individual Churches together in synods and particular councils and especially in episcopal conferences. The second part treats the divisions of ecclesiastical provinces and the erection of ecclesiastical regions. The third and final part deals with the bishops who are entrusted with an interdiocesan mission and who are thus at the service of several particular Churches.

I. Synods, Particular Councils and Episcopal Conferences

This part of the Decree begins by presenting a few brief historical considerations. From the first centuries of the Church, the bishops of certain regions met to take common action either to define, defend and teach the truths of faith, or to make sure that a uniform discipline was observed in the various individual Churches of a particular region. Thus there arose synods, provincial councils and later plenary councils, which were usually national councils.[1] These synods and provincial councils have been maintained, and their structure and functions are regulated by the Canon Law now in effect. More recently cooperation among the bishops of the same region has been brought about in a new institution, namely, episcopal conferences, which have proved their usefulness in practice and are therefore imposed by the present Decree.

1. *Synods and Particular Councils*

Synods and particular councils (that is, provincial councils and plenary councils) are considered in detail in Canon Law. The Council does not change the canonical discipline pertaining to synods and particular councils. It is satisfied with expressing the wish that they flourish again in order to provide for the growth of the faith and the maintenance of ecclesiastical dsicipline in the various particular churches in a way adapted to new circumstances. The revised Code of Canon Law will have to provide for all these demands.

2. *Episcopal Conferences*

Episcopal conferences, as conceived and organized by the present Decree, are a new form of cooperation among bishops of the same region, unknown in the Canon Law in effect up to the present time.

In fact Canon Law provides only for provincial episcopal conferences, as spoken of in Canon 292 of the Code of Canon Law and in Canon 351 of the Motu Proprio *Cleri sanctitati* which was promulgated for the Eastern Churches on June 2, 1957. Unless special regulations are laid down by the Holy See in particular cases, these conferences in the Latin

[1] Cf. A. van Hove, *Prologomena ad Codicem Iuris Canonici* (Malines-Rome, 1945), n. 131, p. 134-35.

Church are composed of the diocesan bishops of a province, as well as those similar to them, and they should meet at least every five years. In the Eastern Churches, they include all the local ordinaries of a province and should meet at least once a year. However, these conferences have only one mission: to discuss the measures to be taken in the different dioceses of the province to promote the good of religion and to prepare the work of a future provincial council or synod. They have no legislative power.

The episcopal conferences provided for by the Decree *Christus Dominus* are something completely different, and they have a different structure and very important competences.

(a) *The Nature of Episcopal Conferences.* According to the text of the Decree (n. 38), these conferences are assemblies in which the prelates of a country or a particular territory exercise their pastoral office together in order to increase the good which the Church offers to men.

Since they bring together only those prelates in charge of particular Churches of the same country or the same territory, they cannot be conceived as a form of exercising the general mission which belongs to the college of bishops. Quite the contrary, they are a new form of exercising together the episcopal power which the bishops possess and exercise for the benefit of the particular Churches entrusted to them. As in the synods or particular councils, so here the bishops exercise the episcopal power of teaching and governing which they rightfully possess in the particular Churches entrusted to them, and which they direct under the authority of the supreme power of the Church, the sovereign pontiff and the college of bishops. As was said above, diocesan bishops are provided in principle with all the ordinary powers demanded by the exercise of the pastoral office in the dioceses entrusted to them. However, since they exercise these powers under the supreme authority of the Church, the latter certainly has the right not only to direct and control the use of the powers, but also to limit their exercise if this be demanded by the good of the universal Church or even of the particular Church. The supreme authority also has the right to determine the ways in which the powers will be exercised. In principle and according to the general rule, the exercise of episcopal power is individual, each bishop exercising proper and ordinary power only for the benefit of the particular Church entrusted to him. Sometimes, however, this power must be exercised together with other bishops. If, in the judgment of the supreme authority of the Church, a uniform regulation is imposed in the various dioceses of the same ecclesiastical province, country or territory, this episcopal power will be exercised collectively in the sense that the bishops in charge of the various dioceses of the province, country or territory will exercise their episcopal power together for the ensemble of dioceses that make up the territory. This is the case in synods and particular councils, whether provincial or plenary. It is also the case in episcopal conferences as conceived by the present Decree. These conferences constitute a new form of the collective exercise of the proper power which the bishops possess insofar as they are in charge of particular Churches.[2]

(b) *The Structure of Episcopal Conferences.* As the Decree indicates, these conferences are as-

[2] Cf. W. Onclin, "Collegiality and the Individual Bishop," in *Concilium,* Vol. 8 (New York: Paulist Press, 1965), pp. 88-89.

semblies of prelates from the same country or territory. In principle they seem to have a national character,[3] but they may also be infranational or even supranational. These last, however, cannot be established without the approval of the Holy See, which alone can prescribe special norms in this case (*Ecclesiae sanctae,* (I, n. 41).

Since the episcopal conferences are a form of the collective exercise of the proper and ordinary power which the bishops hold in their dioceses, it follows that in principle only those bishops in charge of a diocese, and those who are in a position similar to them by being placed in charge as pastors of a group of the faithful, are included in these conferences and take part in them in the exercise of power. Certainly all those who are proper pastors of a diocese or of a group of the faithful are included by right in these conferences. These are patriarchs, metropolitans, diocesan bishops, and those who are likened to them by law: apostolic administrators, prelates or abbots *nullius,* vicars and prefects apostolic, vicars capitular—in a word, all local ordinaries except vicars general and episcopal vicars. All these are by right members of a plenary council (Can. 282, § 1) and a provincial council (Cans. 285 and 286, § 1), and therefore of episcopal conferences.

However, according to the Decree, coadjutor bishops, auxiliary bishops and titular bishops, who exercise in the territory a special function entrusted to them by the Holy See or by episcopal conferences, are also members of these conferences. Coadjutor bishops who are later called to ensure the government of the diocese to which they are attached

[3] This conclusion is drawn from the provisions of the Motu Proprio *Sacram liturgiam,* January 25, 1964, n. 10: *A.A.S.* 56 (1964), p. 143.

have a particular interest in the activity of these conferences. Therefore the Decree grants them a deliberative voice in these conferences. Auxiliary bishops of dioceses, although they are not proper pastors, are bishops and devote all their pastoral activity to the diocese. Titular bishops who fulfill a special function in the territory—for example, as rectors of Catholic universities or directors of a work of the apostolate—are at the service of several or even all the dioceses in the territory. That is why the Decree decided that they are by right members of the conferences. However, they do not have a deliberative voice there unless the statutes of the conference grant it to them. Other titular bishops, residing in a diocese of the territory, and likewise the legates of the sovereign pontiff, are not by right members of episcopal conferences. They can become members if the statutes of the conferences so allow.

There is one conclusion we may draw from these considerations. Coadjutor bishops, as well as auxiliary and titular bishops, to whom the conference grants a deliberative voice, even though they are not proper pastors of a diocese, exercise together with the diocesan bishops the powers granted to the episcopal conferences for the benefit of the dioceses included in the territory of the conferences. Thus the Decree introduces a new form for the exercise of the power proper to diocesan bishops.

Regarding the structure of these conferences, the Decree directs the conferences themselves to draw up their statutes. These must, however, be submitted to the Holy See. Among other things, these statutes should provide for the various organizations that enable the conferences to fulfill their purpose, as, for example: a permanent council to ensure that the prescriptions enacted by the general assembly are carried out; special episcopal commissions in charge of studying certain problems; a general secretariat.

(c) *The Competence of Episcopal Conferences.* The schema "On Bishops and the Government of Dioceses" provided that decisions made in the conferences by a two-thirds majority would entail a juridical obligation for the bishops in four cases: (1) when the deciding of certain cases is allotted to the conferences by common law or by a special mandate from the apostolic see; (2) when the case concerns important declarations to be made publicly in the name of the national conference of bishops; (3) in all cases in which questions of interest to the entire nation are treated with the government of the State; and finally (4) whenever, because of the importance of a question, a common decision is demanded, and, in the opinion of two-thirds of the voting members, the decision taken should have juridical value.

These provisions were the object of much lively discussion in the aula. Certain fathers were resolutely opposed to the granting of some legislative competence to episcopal conferences. They were afraid that the conferral of such competence on the conferences would limit too much the power of the bishops. There was even one father who claimed that such a concession was contrary to divine law; he allowed for no intermediary between the sovereign pontiff and the bishops, who could be subject only to the Roman pontiff. Evidently he forgot about the existence of synods and particular councils. A greater number of the Council fathers were of the opinion that the conferences might enjoy legislative competence in certain cases, but these would be the exception. The conciliar commission therefore reduced the number of these cases in keeping with the wish of the majority of the fathers. That is how the present text regarding the competence of the conferences was drawn up. This text proved satisfactory to the majority of the fathers.

In principle, decisions made by episcopal conferences involve no juridical obligation at all to submit. These decisions do not in principle have the force of ecclesiastical law for the dioceses in the territory of the conferences. Of course the bishops can make certain decisions in common and then, each in his own diocese, can give them the force of law. These would then be the object of diocesan laws and not laws emanating from the episcopal conference itself.

In exceptional cases, however, episcopal conferences are endowed with legislative power and can therefore make decisions which have the force of law and involve the juridical obligation to obey. They can make decisions having this binding force only in matters which belong to their competence in virtue of common law or of a special mandate from the apostolic see. However, this mandate can also be given at the request of the conference itself. For the decisions taken by the conferences in such cases to have obligatory force, however, they must be approved by at least two-thirds of the prelates having a deliberative voice in the conference, and must be submitted to and acknowledged by the Holy See.

The decisions thus taken by episcopal conferences are canon laws coming from the conferences. In fact, in these conferences, as in synods and particular councils, the bishops do not exercise a power they have from the sovereign pontiff, but exercise together the episcopal power that belongs to them. Naturally, to have the force of law, the decisions of the conferences, like the decrees of synods and particular councils (Can. 291, § 1; *Cleri sanctitati,* Can. 350, § 1), must be *recognitae* ("acknowledged") by the Holy See. But this *recognitio* is not *approbatio,* and signifies only that the decisions or decrees must be submitted to the Holy See and receive its signature.[4] It does not constitute a specific approval of these decisions, and does not change their juridical character. By means of this *recognitio,* these decisions do not become decisions of the Holy See, but remain measures taken by the bishops themselves exercising together the episcopal power which belongs to them and which they hold for the benefit of the particular churches in their charge.[5]

(d) *Cooperation among Episcopal Conferences.* The Decree encourages the conferences of different countries to establish relations among themselves in order to promote and ensure a greater good for all concerned. Whenever these relations result in some common action of an international nature, however, the Holy See must be informed (*Ecclesiae sanctae,* I, n. 41).

Along the same line, the Decree, at the end of this section, declares that, in territories where Churches of different rites are established, the synods of Oriental Churches should seek to promote the common good of the entire territory by organizing interritual meetings in accordance with norms drawn up by the competent authority.

---

[4] Cf. R. Naz. *Traité de droit canonique,* Vol. I (Paris, 1954), n. 587, p. 420.

[5] Cf. W. Onclin, *art. cit.,* pp. 90-91.

II. Boundaries of Ecclesiastical Provinces and the Erection of Ecclesiastical Regions

The question of the division of ecclesiastical provinces was treated in the schema "On the Bishops and the Government of Dioceses" together with that on the division of dioceses. In the present Decree it is separated from the latter and included in Chapter III, which deals with cooperation among bishops of the same ecclesiastical province or country. This is certainly more logical, since ecclesiastical provinces are established to promote cooperation among bishops of the same region. The rules laid down by the Decree regarding ecclesiastical provinces are as follows: (a) ecclesiastical provinces should be revised in view of the present needs of the apostolate; (b) the rights and privileges of metropolitans should be defined by suitable norms; (c) in general, all dioceses, as well as all territorial jurisdictions equivalent to them, should henceforth become part of some ecclesiastical province, so that there will no longer by any dioceses called exempt, immediately subject to the Holy See.

The question of erecting ecclesiastical regions was not taken up by the schema "On Bishops and the Government of Dioceses". It became necessary, however, since closer relations among bishops of the same country or region (relations recommended by the Decree) would certainly be fostered by the canonical creation and organization of ecclesiastical regions. The Decree does not enforce their erection, but provides that they be erected wherever it appears useful to do so, and that their organization be determined by law. These ecclesiastical regions are territorial, national or regional jurisdictions, which are made up of several ecclesiastical provinces, but, like them, at least in the present legislation, they are not moral persons and are only administrative districts.

Questions concerning the division of ecclesiastical provinces and the erection of ecclesiastical regions should be studied by the various interested episcopal conferences, which should be guided by the norms established for the division of dioceses and should submit their opinions and wishes to the Holy See.

III. Bishops Engaged in an Interdiocesan Mission

The third part of this chapter concerns bishops who carry out interdiocesan functions. This matter was not considered in the schema "On Bishops and the Government of Dioceses", which, as we have said, was concerned primarily with bishops in the government of dioceses. But the Council wanted this Decree to deal with the entire episcopal mission and to consider all the apostolic duties which could be entrusted to bishops in the Church. The *Decree on the Pastoral Office of Bishops in the Church* therefore speaks of those bishops who are neither diocesan nor coadjutors nor auxiliaries attached to a particular diocese, but fulfill important functions in the service of the faithful of different dioceses in the same region or country. Especially in modern times, there are certain works of the apostolate that demand an interdiocesan organization. Those in charge of such works —and they are often bishops—fulfill an apostolic office in the service of various particular Churches. In order to fulfill this office effectively, they should cooperate with the diocesan bishops in charge of the dioceses concerned with their activity. The conditions of this cooperation are to be determined by common law.

The Decree makes special mention of the vicars for the armed forces, called *vicarii castrenses,* who have already been established in many countries. The Decree asks that, whenever possible, these be established in each country, and it directs the diocesan bishops to provide a sufficient number of priests who have the qualities demanded for the fulfillment of this difficult work.

The Final Statement of the Decree

The general statement which concludes the Decree first of all directs the pontifical Commission for the Revision of the Code of Canon Law to carry out this revision in keeping with the principles set forth in the present Decree and with the observations expressed by the commissions and the fathers of the Council. Furthermore, as Pope Paul VI said in his allocution to the cardinal members and consultors of this commission on November 20, 1965, Canon Law should be adapted to the new spirit of Vatican Council II and the work of revising the Code should develop further and apply the principles established by this Council.[6]

The general statement also orders the drawing up of general directories on pastoral care for the use of bishops and pastors. A directory should also be prepared on the pastoral care of certain special groups of the faithful, taking into account the special conditions of different countries. There should also be a directory on the catechetical instruction

---

[6] Cf. *A.A.S.* 57 (1965), pp. 985-89.

of the Christian people, giving the fundamental principles for organizing this teaching and preparing books on the subject. The Decree does not specify who is in charge of these directories, but states that those handling this task should take into account the observations made by the commissions and fathers of the Council.

Conclusion

From this brief analysis of its chief provisions, we can see that the Decree *Christus Dominus* is certainly an important document in the life of the Church. As was said above, this Decree extends and puts into practice the theology set forth in the Dogmatic Constitution *Lumen gentium*. This theology must be put into practice, and it will be so only by the decisive impulse given to the life of the Church by the bishops, who were established by Christ to direct his Church.

Naturally the present Decree does not solve all the questions raised concerning the pastoral office entrusted to bishops in the Church. It does constitute a new and important document, however, in which pastoral considerations are dominant. It also calls for the study of many questions concerning pastoral care, and the bishops will be eager to promote this study. Putting it into practice will demand many different methods and procedures. It will especially demand the active cooperation of pastors, whose duties, no less than their rights and powers, are determined by the Decree. It will also demand the understanding and goodwill of priests, religious and faithful, whose cooperation is absolutely necessary if the pastors are to fulfill their difficult task.

Study-Club Questions

1. How are episcopal conferences a new form of cooperation among bishops?
2. Who may participate in episcopal conferences?
3. Do episcopal conferences have any legislative power? Explain.
4. Must all the decisions of episcopal conferences be approved by the pope? Explain.
5. What is the difference between an ecclesiastical province and a diocese?
6. Mention some apostolic works that require interdiocesan organization.
7. What is the difference between an ecclesiastical province and an ecclesiastical region?
8. Mention three ways in which bishops can cooperate for the common good of many Churches.
9. What is an episcopal synod?
10. What is a provincial council?
11. Does Canon Law make any provision for provincial episcopal conferences? Explain.

12. Explain the following terms: (1) patriarch; (2) metropolitan; (3) abbot *nullius;* (4) apostolic administrator; (5) prefect apostolic.

13. Are you obliged to obey all the decisions of episcopal conferences? Explain.

14. Mention five apostolic duties that could be entrusted to bishops in the Church.

15. What does this Decree say about the Commission for the Revision of the Code of Canon Law?

16. How many general directories does this Decree urge to be drawn up? What is the value of a general directory?

17. Mention some pastoral problems of bishops that this Decree does not discuss.

18. Mention some pastoral problems that should be considered by episcopal conferences in your area.

19. Briefly discuss three major conclusions of this Decree.

20. What can you do to carry out the provisions of this Decree?

Christus Dominus

THE DECREE ON THE PASTORAL OFFICE OF BISHOPS IN THE CHURCH

Promulgated by Pope Paul VI
October 28, 1965

PAUL BISHOP

SERVANT OF THE SERVANTS OF GOD
TOGETHER WITH THE FATHERS OF THE SACRED COUNCIL
COMMITS TO PERMANENT RECORD

THE DECREE ON THE PASTORAL OFFICE OF BISHOPS IN THE CHURCH

PREFACE

1. Christ the Lord, the Son of the living God, came to save his people from sin [1] and make all men holy. As he was sent by the Father, so he sent his apostles,[2] whom he sanctified by conferring the Holy Spirit on them, that they mighty glorify the Father on earth and work for the salvation of men "to the building up of the body of Christ" (Eph. 4, 12), which is the Church.

2. In this Church of Christ, the Roman pontiff has, by divine right as the successor of Peter to whom Christ entrusted the task of feeding his lambs and his sheep, supreme, full, immediate and universal power in the care of souls. Therefore, he who has been sent as the pastor of all the faithful to

[1] Cf. Mt. 1, 21.
[2] Cf. Jn. 20, 21.

ensure the common good of the whole Church, and the good of individual Churches, has supreme ordinary power over all the Churches.

Having been appointed by the Holy Spirit, bishops succeed the apostles as pastors of souls; [3] they have been sent, in union with the supreme pontiff and subject to his authority, to perpetuate the work of Christ, the eternal pastor.[4] Christ gave his apostles and their successors the command and the power to teach all nations, to sanctify men in truth and to nourish them. Thus, through the Holy Spirit who has been given to them, the bishops have become the true and authentic teachers, pontiffs and pastors of the faith.[5]

3. Bishops share in the care of all the Churches and exercise their episcopal office, which they took on by episcopal consecration,[6] in communion with the pope and under his authority. As regards the Church of God as a whole, in all that concerns the magisterium and pastoral government, they are all united in a college or body.

With reference to the portions of the Lord's flock which have been entrusted to them, they carry out this task individually, each of them taking care of the particular Church committed to him. At times some of them may together provide for certain needs common to a number of separate Churches.

Therefore, this sacred Synod, conscious of the condition of human society which in our time is

---

[3] Cf. Vatican Council I, *Dogmatic Constitution on the Church of Christ*, Ch. 3: *Denz.* 1828 (3061).

[4] Cf. Vatican Council I, *Dogmatic Constitution on the Church of Christ*, Introduction: *Denz.* 1821 (3050).

[5] Cf. Vatican Council II, *Dogmatic Constitution on the Church*, nn. 21, 24, 25: *A.A.S.* 57 (1965), pp. 24-25, 29-31.

[6] Cf. *ibid.*, n. 21.

moving toward a new order of things,[7] and wishing to determine in a more precise way the pastoral office of bishops, has decided to promulgate what here follows.

---

[7] Cf. John XXIII, Apostolic Constitution *Humanae salutis*, Dec. 25, 1961: *A.A.S.* 54 (1962), p. 6.

Chapter I

Bishops and the Universal Church

I. Role of Bishops in the Universal Church

4. Bishops are constituted members of the episcopal body by sacramental consecration and hierarchical communion with the head and members of the college.[8] "The order of bishops which succeeds the college of the apostles in its office of teaching and pastoral government, and as that in which the apostolic body endures without interruption, is also, together with its head, the Roman pontiff, and never without this head, the subject of supreme and plenary power over the whole Church, but this power cannot be exercised without the consent of the Roman pontiff." [9] This power "is solemnly exercised in an ecumenical Council".[10] Therefore, this Council decrees that all bishops who are members of the episcopal college have the right to take part in an ecumenical Council.

"This same collegiate power can be exercised, in union with the pope, by bishops residing throughout the world, provided the head of the

[8] Cf. Vatican Council II, *Dogmatic Constitution on the Church,* n. 22: *A.A.S.* 57 (1965), pp. 25-27.

[9] Cf. *ibid.*

[10] Cf. *ibid.*

college calls them to exercise collegiate action, or at least approves of the common action, or freely accepts it, so that it becomes a true act of collegiality."[11]

5. Bishops chosen from different parts of the world, in a manner and according to norms laid down or to be laid down by the Roman pontiff, render more effective assistance to the supreme pastor of the Church in that body which is called the synod of bishops.[12] This synod, while representing the whole Catholic episcopate, is likewise a sign that all bishops, by a hierarchical communion, share in the care of the whole Church.[13]

6. As the legitimate successors of the apostles and members of the episcopal college, bishops should realize that they are always bound together and so should show themselves to be concerned for all the Churches; by divine institution and by reason of the obligations of the apostolic office, each one of them, in union with the other bishops, is responsible for the Church.[14] They should be especially concerned for those parts of the world where the Word of God has not yet been preached, or in which, due mainly to the small number of priests, the faithful are in danger of straying from the precepts of the Christian life, and even of losing the faith itself.

---

[11] Cf. *ibid.*

[12] Cf. Paul VI, Motu Proprio *Apostolica sollicitudo,* Sept. 15, 1965.

[13] Cf. Vatican Council II, *Dogmatic Constitution on the Church,* n. 23: *A.A.S.* 57 (1965), pp. 27-28.

[14] Cf. Pius XII, Encyclical Letter *Fidei donum,* April 21, 1957: *A.A.S.* 49 (1957), pp. 237ff.; also cf. Benedict XV, Apostolic Letter *Maximum illud,* Nov. 30, 1919: *A.A.S.* 11 (1919), p. 440; Pius XI, Encyclical Letter *Rerum Ecclesiae,* Feb. 28, 1926: *A.A.S.* 18 (1926), p. 68.

They must therefore make every effort to ensure that the work of evangelization and of the apostolate is zealously supported and fostered by the faithful. They should likewise see to it that worthy ministers, as well as religious and lay helpers, are trained for the missions and regions that are short of clergy. Insofar as it is possible, they should try to ensure that some of their own priests go to these missions or dioceses and there carry out the sacred ministry either permanently or at least for a set period.

In the use of Church property bishops should be conscious not only of the needs of their own dioceses, but also of the needs of other Churches, since they are part of the one Church of Christ. Finally, they should make every effort to help other dioceses or regions whenever calamities may come upon them.

7. Let them especially embrace with brotherly affection those bishops who are victims of calumnies and persecutions for the name of Christ, those who are in prison or forbidden to exercise their ministry; they should have an active brotherly concern for these men so that their sufferings might be lightened and relieved by the prayers and good works of their colleagues.

II. Bishops and the Apostolic See

8. In the dioceses which have been entrusted to them, bishops, as the successors of the apostles, have *per se* all the ordinary, proper and immediate power that is necessary for the exercise of their pastoral duty; however, the power which the Roman pontiff has in all matters, in virtue of his office, to reserve cases to himself or to some other

authority must always be safeguarded. Every diocesan bishop has the faculty in particular cases to dispense the faithful, over whom he has lawful authority, from a general law of the Church, as often as he judges that it will contribute to their spiritual good, unless the case has been especially reserved by the supreme authority of the Church.

9. In exercising his supreme, full and immediate power over the universal Church, the Roman pontiff avails himself of the congregations of the Roman Curia, which therefore in his name and with his authority carry out their duties for the good of the churches and in the service of their pastors.

However, the fathers of the Council desire that these congregations, which have rendered outstanding service to the Roman pontiff and to the pastors of the Church, should be reorganized in a manner that is more in keeping with the needs of the times and of the various regions and rites, especially as regards their number, name, competence, individual manner of procedure and coordination of their work.[15] They also desire, in view of the pastoral office of bishops, that the function of papal legates should be more accurately defined.

10. Also, since the congregations were instituted for the good of the whole Church, it is desirable that their personnel, officials and consultors, as well as legates of the Roman pontiff, should, as far as possible, be more frequently taken from different regions of the Church, so that the offices or central organs of the Catholic Church will present a truly universal character.

Finally, the fathers of the Council think that it would be extremely advantageous if these congrega-

---

[15] Cf. Paul VI, *Allocution to the Cardinals, Prelates and Various Officials of the Roman Curia,* Sept. 21, 1963: *A.A.S.* 55 (1963), pp. 793ff.

tions consulted lay people more often, people who are renowned for virtue, knowledge and experience, so that they, too, might play an appropriate part in the affairs of the Church.

Study-Club Questions

1. How do bishops help to "build up the body of Christ"?

2. By what right does the Roman pontiff have supreme ordinary power over all the Churches?

3. Bishops are "true and authentic teachers, pontiffs and pastors of the faith." Explain.

4. What is the purpose of this Decree?

5. What does n. 22 of the *Constitution on the Church* tell us about the power of bishops?

6. Briefly discuss the two different ways in which collegiate power is exercised.

7. How is the synod of bishops a sign of hierarchical communion?

8. Why is each individual bishop responsible for the welfare of the whole Church?

9. Are bishops reponsible for the welfare of the non-Christian world? Explain.

10. How should bishops use Church property?

11. How can bishops help their fellow bishops who are being persecuted and imprisoned throughout the world?

12. Why should there be any dispensations from a general law of the Church?

13. What does this Decree specifically recommend for the reorganization of the congregations of the Roman curia?

14. What kind of lay people should participate in the work of the Roman curia?

15. What does n. 21 of the *Constitution on the Church* tell us about episcopal consecration?

16. Why is Vatican Council II called a "sacred Synod"?

17. Can bishops ever exercise supreme and plenary power without the authority of the pope? Explain.

18. How can bishops help those parts of the Church that have very few priests?

19. How do the congregations of the Roman curia help the pope?

20. What can you do to help the missionary activity of the Church?

Chapter II

Bishops and Particular Churches or Dioceses

I. Diocesan Bishops

11. A diocese is a portion of the People of God which is entrusted to a bishop to be cared for with the assistance of his presbyterium, so that adhering to its pastor, and gathered together by him in the Holy Spirit through the Gospel and the eucharist, it might form a particular church in which the one, holy, catholic and apostolic Church of Christ is really present and active.

Individual bishops, to whom the care of a particular Church has been committed subject to the authority of the pope, as the proper, ordinary and immediate pastors of their people, feed their sheep in the name of the Lord by exercising the office of teaching, sanctifying and governing in their regard. They should, however, recognize the rights which belong legitimately to patriarchs or other hierarchical authorities.[16]

Bishops should dedicate themselves to their apostolic office as witnesses of Christ before all men.

---

[16] Cf. Vatican Council II, *Decree on the Catholic Churches of the Eastern Rite,* Nov. 21, 1964, nn. 7-11: *A.A.S.* 57 (1965), pp. 79-80.

They should not merely care for those who already follow the prince of pastors, but should also consecrate themselves wholeheartedly to those who have in any way strayed from the path of truth, or who have no knowledge of the Gospel and the saving mercy of Christ. This they should do until finally all men walk "in all goodness and justice and truth" (Eph. 5, 9).

12. In carrying out their office of teaching, let them proclaim the Gospel of Christ to men (a preeminent duty of bishops),[17] either calling them to the faith in the power of the Spirit, or else strengthening them in an already living faith. They should place before them the full mystery of Christ—namely, those truths, the ignorance of which involves ignorance of Christ. They should likewise show them the divinely revealed way of glorifying God and of thus attaining eternal happiness.[18]

They should show, too, that the things of this world and human institutions can also, in the plan of the creator, be ordered to the salvation of men and so can greatly contribute to the building up of the body of Christ.

In keeping with the doctrine of the Church, they should teach them the true value of the human person with his freedom and bodily life, of the family with its unity and stability, of the procreation and education of children, of civil society with its laws and professions, of work and leisure, of the arts and technical progress, of poverty and affluence. They should explain how very grave problems regarding the ownership, increase and proper distri-

---

[17] Cf. Council of Trent, *Decree on Reforms,* Ch. 2: *Mansi* 33, 30 and 159; cf. also Vatican Council II *Dogmatic Constitution on the Church,* n. 25: *A.A.S.* 57 (1965), pp. 29ff.

[18] Cf. Vatican Council II, *Dogmatic Constitution on the Church,* n. 25: *A.A.S.* 57 (1965), pp. 29-31.

bution of material goods are to be resolved, as well as related questions concerning peace and war and brotherly relations among all peoples.[19]

13. Bishops should expound Christian doctrine in a manner that is adapted to the needs of the times, one that will answer the difficulties and problems which most trouble and oppress men; they should guard that doctrine and teach the faithful to defend and spread it. In this teaching they should manifest the maternal concern of the Church for all men, whether believers or non-believers, and they should care especially for the poor and weak whom the Lord sent them to evangelize.

Since the Church must enter into dialogue with the human society in which she lives,[20] it is especially the duty of bishops to approach men and to seek and promote dialogue with them. In order that it might combine truth with charity and understanding with love, this dialogue of salvation should be noted for clarity of language as well as humility and mildness, as well as for due prudence combined with trust; all of these foster friendship and are, therefore, likely to bring about a union of minds.[21]

They should endeavor to make use of the various means available today for proclaiming Christian doctrine, especially preaching and catechetical instruction which always hold pride of place, but also by its exposition in schools and academies, at conferences and gatherings of all kinds, and by its diffusion in public statements made on special occasions. Full use should be made of the press and

---

[19] Cf. John XXIII, Encyclical Letter *Pacem in terris,* April 11, 1963, *passim*: *A.A.S.* 55 (1963), pp. 257-304.

[20] Cf. Paul VI, Encyclical Letter *Ecclesiam suam,* Aug. 6, 1964: *A.A.S.* 56 (1964), p. 639.

[21] Cf. *ibid.,* pp. 644-45.

other media of communication in proclaiming the Gospel of Christ.[22]

14. As regards catechetical instruction, which has the effect on men of making their faith, illumined by doctrine, something living, explicit and active, bishops should be watchful that it is given with great care to children, adolescents, youths and even adults. They should also ensure that a right order is observed in imparting this instruction and that the method employed is adapted not only to the matter being considered, but also to the mentality, ability, age and manner of life of those being instructed. They should see to it that this instruction is based on sacred scripture, tradition, the liturgy and the magisterium and life of the Church.

They should also take care that catechists are properly prepared for their task so that they will clearly understand the teaching of the Church and have both a theoretical and practical knowledge of the laws of psychology and pedagogical method. They should also try to revise, or more suitably adapt, the instruction of adult catechumens.

15. In carrying out their work of sanctifying, bishops should remember that they have been chosen from among men and appointed to act on their behalf before God in order to offer gifts and sacrifices for sins. Bishops possess the fullness of the sacrament of orders, and both presbyters and deacons depend on them in the exercise of their power. Presbyters have been consecrated as true priests of the New Testament so that they might be prudent fellow-workers of the episcopal order; deacons, having been ordained for the ministry, serve the People of God in communion with the bishop and his presbyterium. Therefore, the bishops are the principal

---

[22] Cf. Vatican Council II, *Decree on the Media of Social Communications,* Dec. 4, 1963: *A.A.S.* 56 (1964), pp. 145-53.

stewards of the mysteries of God; they are likewise the organizers, promoters and guardians of the whole liturgical life of that Church which has been entrusted to them.[23]

Therefore, they should always make every effort to ensure that the faithful fully understand and live the paschal mystery by means of the eucharist so that they might form a closely-knit body in the unity of the charity of Christ; [24] "intent upon prayer and the ministry of the Word" (Acts 6, 4) they should labor that all who have been committed to their care might be of one mind in prayer,[25] grow in grace through the reception of the sacraments and be faithful witnesses to the Lord.

As teachers of perfection, bishops must take care to advance the sanctity of their clerics, religious and laity, each according to his own vocation,[26] being mindful, indeed, that they are themselves bound to give an example of sanctity by their charity, humility and simplicity of life. They should likewise sanctify the Churches entrusted to them that they might fully manifest the spirit of the universal Church of Christ. To this end they should make every effort to foster vocations to the priesthood and the religious life, especially missionary vocations.

16. In exercising their office of father and pastor, bishops should be in the midst of their people as

---

[23] Cf. Vatican Council II, *Constitution on the Sacred Liturgy*, Dec. 4, 1963: *A.A.S.* 56 (1964), pp. 97ff.; Paul VI, Motu Proprio *Sacram liturgiam*, Jan. 25, 1964: *A.A.S.* 56 (1964), pp. 139ff.

[24] Cf. Pius XII, Encyclical Letter *Mediator Dei*, Nov. 20, 1947: *A.A.S.* 39 (1947), pp. 251ff.; Paul VI, Encyclical Letter *Mysterium fidei*, Sept. 3, 1965.

[25] Cf. Acts 1, 14; 2, 46.

[26] Cf. Vatican Council II, *Dogmatic Constitution on the Church*, nn. 44-45: *A.A.S.* 57 (1965), pp. 50-52.

those who serve,[27] good shepherds who know their sheep and whose sheep know them, true fathers, renowned for their spirit of love and solicitude for all, to whose divinely bestowed authority all gratefully submit themselves. They should so assemble and form the whole family of their flock, that all, being conscious of their duties, might live and work in a communion of love.

In order that they might effectively accomplish these things, bishops, "ready for every good work" (2 Tim. 2, 21) and "enduring all things for the sake of the chosen ones" (2 Tim. 2, 10), should regulate their lives in a manner that is in keeping with the needs of the times.

Bishops should always have a special love for priests, since priests relieve them of some of their duties and responsibilities and zealously and carefully fulfill them day by day. They should regard them as sons and friends[28] and always be prepared to listen to them; they should establish a relationship of trust with them and strive to promote the entire pastoral work of the whole diocese.

They should be concerned for their spiritual, intellectual and material welfare so that they might be enabled to live good and holy lives and fulfill their ministry faithfully and fruitfully. For this reason they should encourage institutes and organize special congresses where priests might come from time to time for the purpose of more prolonged retreats ordered to a renewal of life and to acquire a deeper understanding of ecclesiastical studies, especially sacred scripture, theology, the more important social problems and new approaches to pastoral work. They must have an active compassion for those priests who are in danger in some way or

[27] Cf. Lk. 22, 26-27.
[28] Cf. Jn. 15, 15.

another, or who may have failed in certain matters.

In order to better provide for the welfare of the faithful, each according to his state, bishops should make every effort to rightly understand their needs in the social context in which they live by availing themselves of the proper means, especially social research. They should show themselves to be concerned for all men, whatever their age, condition or nationality, whether they are natives of the place, strangers or travelers. In the exercise of this pastoral concern they should reserve for the faithful that part which is theirs in the affairs of the Church, recognizing their obligation and their right to work for the building up of the mystical body of Christ.

They should love the separated brethren and advise the faithful to act toward them with great kindness and charity; they should foster ecumenism as it is understood by the Church.[29] They should also be concerned for the non-baptized, so that the charity of Christ, whose witnesses they are before all men, might shine upon these people.

17. The various forms of the apostolate should be fostered. Throughout the entire diocese, and in particular areas of it, there should be a coordination and close linking together, under the direction of the bishop, of all apostolic work so that all undertakings and organizations—catechetical, missionary, charitable, social, family, education, or whatever has a pastoral purpose—might be combined in a common effort and so more clearly manifest the unity of the diocese.

The obligation of the faithful to engage in the apostolate, each according to his position and ability, should be strongly emphasized; they should be exhorted to support and participate in the various

[29] Cf. Vatican Council II, *Decree on Ecumenism,* Nov. 21, 1964: *A.A.S.* 57 (1965), pp. 90-107.

works of the lay apostolate, especially Catholic action. Associations which either directly or indirectly pursue some supernatural end should be encouraged and promoted, such as those for the preaching of the Gospel of Christ to all men, for the promotion of Christian doctrine and the increase of public worship, for the living of a more perfect life, for the attaining of certain social ends, or for the exercise of works of either piety or charity.

The forms of the apostolate should be properly adapted to modern needs and should take into account not only men's spiritual and moral condition, but also their social, demographic and economic situation. Social and religious research is a great aid to the effective and fruitful attainment of this end and is highly recommended.

18. Special care must be taken of those faithful who, because of the circumstances of their lives, cannot sufficiently avail themselves of the common and ordinary pastoral care of parish priests, or who are totally deprived of such care. This is the case with most emigrants, exiles, refugees, sailors, those engaged in air travel, nomads and others in similar circumstances. Suitable pastoral efforts should also be made to foster the spiritual life of those who go abroad for a period on holidays.

Conferences of bishops, especially national conferences, should carefully examine the more urgent questions which arise regarding the above-mentioned groups. Through common agreement, united effort and by suitable means and organizations, they should provide for the spiritual care of these people, taking into account, first of all, the norms laid down or to be laid down by the Holy See,[30] while at

---

[30] Cf. St. Pius X, Motu Proprio *Iampridem, March* 19, 1914: *A.A.S.* 6 (1914), pp. 174ff.; Pius XII, Apostolic Constitution *Exsul familia,* Aug. 1, 1952: *A.A.S.* 44 (1952), pp. 652ff.;

the same time suitably adapting them to circumstances of time, place and persons.

19. In the exercise of their apostolic ministry, which is concerned with the salvation of souls, bishops *per se* enjoy full and perfect liberty and independence of all civil authority. Therefore, it is not lawful, either directly or indirectly, to hinder the exercise of their ecclesiastical office or to forbid them free communication with the apostolic see, with other ecclesiastical authorities or with their own subjects.

By devoting themselves to the spiritual care of their flock, bishops also truly contribute to social and civil progress and prosperity by actively cooperating with the civil authorities to this end, insofar as it is in keeping with the nature of their office and proper for them to do so, and also by advocating obedience to just laws and respect for legitimately constituted authority.

20. Since the apostolic office of bishops was instituted by Christ the Lord, and since it is directed toward a spiritual and supernatural end, this ecumenical Council declares that the right to nominate and institute bishops is proper, peculiar and *per se* exclusive to the competent ecclesiastical authority.

Therefore, in order to protect the freedom of the Church and more effectively promote the welfare of Christians, it is the will of the Council that civil authorities should never in the future be granted the right or privilege of election, nomination, presentation or designation with regard to the episcopal office. Civil authorities, whose respect for the Church this sacred Synod gratefully recognizes and appreciates, are graciously asked, after consultation with the Holy See, to freely forego the

---

Leges operis apostolatus maris, compiled under the authority of Pius XII, Nov. 21, 1957: *A.A.S.* 50 (1958), pp. 375ff.

aforesaid rights and privileges which they may presently enjoy by reason of some pact or custom.

21. Since the pastoral office of bishops is of such importance and gravity, diocesan bishops, and those equivalent to them in law, are earnestly asked to offer their resignation from office, either on their own initiative or when invited by the competent authority, if because of old age or for some other serious reason they become less capable of carrying out their office. If the competent authority accepts the resignation, it will provide for the proper support of those who resign and ensure that they are accorded special rights.

II. Diocesan Boundaries

22. If the precise purpose of the diocese is to be attained, then the People of God who make up that diocese should clearly manifest the nature of the Church. Bishops should be able to effectively carry out their pastoral duties in the diocese, and the salvation of the People of God must be served in the most perfect manner possible.

This requires not only a suitable adjustment of the territorial boundaries of dioceses but also a rational distribution of clergy and resources, and one that is adapted to the needs of the apostolate. This will not only benefit the clergy and faithful who are directly concerned, but will be for the good of the whole Catholic Church.

Therefore, with regard to the boundaries of dioceses, the Council decrees that, insofar as it is necessary for the good of souls, a suitable revision should be prudently undertaken as soon as possible. This can be done by dividing dioceses, breaking them up, amalgamating them, changing their boundaries, finding a more appropriate place for the episcopal see, or, finally, especially if it is a case of dioceses which contain large cities, by internal reorganization.

23. As if it were a living body, the first thing which must be safeguarded in revising the boundaries of any diocese is its organic unity as regards personnel, offices and institutions. In each case, after carefully considering all the circumstances, the following general norms should be kept in mind.

(a) In determining the diocesan boundary, consideration should be given as far as possible to the various elements which go to make up the People of God, as this will greatly assist the better exercise of pastoral care. At the same time care should be taken so that the unity between centers of population and the civil offices and social institutions which constitute their organic structure is maintained. For this reason the territory of each diocese should be continuous.

If necessary, civil boundaries should also be taken into consideration, as well as special circumstances affecting places or groups. These circumstances may, for example, be economic, geographic or historical.

(b) The territorial extent of a diocese and the number of its inhabitants should generally be such that the bishop, even though assisted by others, can personally officiate at pontifical ceremonies, conveniently make pastoral visitations, effectively direct and coordinate all the works of the apostolate in the diocese and, above all, know his priests and those religious and lay people who are engaged in diocesan undertakings. On the other hand, conscious of the needs of the universal Church, it should provide an adequate and suitable field of activity, one in which both bishop and clergy will be able to expend all their energies usefully in the work of the ministry.

(c) Finally, as a general rule, in order that the ministry of salvation might be more effectively carried out, there should be in each diocese a clergy sufficiently numerous and qualified to properly care for the People of God; it should not lack the offices, institutions and works which are proper to a particular Church and which experience has proved to be necessary for an effective government and apostolate. Lastly, the diocese should already possess, or at least be prudently assured of acquiring elsewhere, the resources necessary to support diocesan personnel and institutions.

Whenever there are faithful of different rites, the diocesan bishop should provide for their spiritual needs either through priests or parishes of the same rite, or by an episcopal vicar possessing the requisite faculties, or even, if necessary, by one who is also a consecrated bishop; the bishop himself may fulfill the office of ordinary of the different rites. If, in the judgment of the Holy See, all this cannot be done for some special reason, then a separate hierarchy for the different rites is to be established.[31]

Likewise, in similar circumstances, provisions should be made for the faithful of different language groups, either through priests or parishes of the same language, or by an episcopal vicar who speaks the language well (and who could, if necessary, be a bishop), or in some other more suitable way.

24. In order to bring about the changes and alterations mentioned in nn. 22-23, it is desirable that the competent episcopal conferences examine these

---

[31] Cf. Vatican Council II, *Decree on the Catholic Churches of the Eastern Rite*, Nov. 21, 1964, n. 4: *A.A.S.* 57 (1965), p. 77.

matters, each with regard to its own territory, without, however, infringing on the discipline of the Oriental churches. If it seems opportune, they can set up a special episcopal commission, but they must, above all, always consult the bishops of the provinces or regions in question. Finally, they should submit their recommendations and desires to the apostolic see.

III. Assistants of the Diocesan Bishop in the Pastoral Office

25. In the governing of dioceses, the pastoral office of bishops should be provided for in such a manner that the good of the Lord's flock is always the supreme consideration. In order that this good be properly achieved, it is often necessary to appoint auxiliary bishops, either because the diocesan bishop is unable personally to carry out all the episcopal functions necessary for the good of souls, or because of the extent of the dioceses, too great a number of inhabitants, special circumstances of the apostolate, or other reasons. At times, indeed, some special circumstance may demand that a coadjutor bishop be appointed as assistant to the diocesan bishop. These coadjutors and auxiliaries are to be given suitable faculties so that, without detriment to the unity of the diocese and the authority of the bishop, their work may be more effective and the dignity proper to bishops rendered more secure.

Furthermore, coadjutor and auxiliary bishops, since they are called to share the responsibilities of the diocesan bishop, should always carry out their task in harmony with him. They should at all times show obedience and respect for the diocesan bishop, and he, on his part, should love them as brothers and treat them with respect.

26. Whenever it is necessary for the good of souls, the diocesan bishop should be prepared to ask the competent authority for one or more auxiliaries who would thereupon be appointed for the diocese without the right of succession.

If it is not provided for by the letters of nomination, the diocesan bishop should appoint his auxiliary, or auxiliaries, as vicars general, or at least as episcopal vicars, dependent on his authority. He should consult them in the more important matters, especially those of a pastoral nature.

Unless otherwise determined by the competent authority, the powers and faculties which auxiliary bishops have by law do not expire with the diocesan bishop. When the see is vacant, it is desirable that the task of ruling the diocese should be committed to the auxiliary bishop, or to one of them where there are many, unless serious reasons suggest otherwise.

A coadjutor bishop—that is, one nominated with the right of succession—must always be appointed vicar general by the diocesan bishop. In special cases he can be granted wider faculties by the competent authority. For the greater good of the diocese, both now and in the future, the diocesan bishop and his coadjutor should not omit to consult together on matters of greater importance.

27. The most important office in the diocesan curia is that of vicar general. However, whenever it is necessary for the proper administration of the diocese, one or more episcopal vicars may be appointed by the bishop. By law these will have the same power in a particular part of the diocese, or in some special matters, or for the faithful of a par-

ticular rite, as is given to the vicar general by the common law.

Among the assistants of the bishop in the administration of the diocese are those priests who constitute his senate or council, such as the cathedral chapter, groups of consultors or other councils, according to the circumstances of various places. Wherever necessary, these institutions, especially cathedral chapters, should be reorganized in keeping with present-day requirements.

Priests and lay people who belong to the diocesan curia should realize that they are making a useful contribution to the pastoral ministry of the bishop.

The diocesan curia should be so organized that it will become a suitable instrument in the hands of the bishop not only for administering the diocese, but also for carrying out the works of the apostolate.

It is greatly to be desired that a special pastoral council be set up on each diocese over which the bishop would preside and in which specially chosen clergy, religious and lay people would have a part. The task of this council would be to study and examine whatever has to do with pastoral activities and to formulate practical conclusions in their regard.

28. All priests, whether diocesan or religious, share with the bishop in the one priesthood of Christ and are therefore appointed as the prudent co-workers of the episcopal order. Diocesan priests have the principal role in the care of souls because they are incardinated or attached to a particular church; they give themselves fully to its service in order to tend this one portion of the Lord's flock. They constitute one priestly body (presbyterium) and one family, of which the bishop is the head. In

order to allot the various sacred ministries among his priests more fittingly and fairly, the bishop should have the necessary freedom in conferring benefices and offices. Rights and privileges which in any way restrict this freedom are to be abolished.

Relations between the bishop and the priests of the diocese should be based primarily on bonds of supernatural charity so that the unity of priests and bishop might make their pastoral work more fruitful. Therefore, in order that the service of souls might be increasingly advanced, the bishop should invite his priests to discuss matters with him, even in common, especially pastoral questions. He should do this not only when the need arises, but even at set times if possible.

Furthermore, all the diocesan priests should be united among themselves and feel urged on by their responsibility for the spiritual good of the whole diocese. Mindful of the fact that the goods which they obtain by reason of their ecclesiastical office are closely connected with their sacred ministry, they should generously and according to their means support the material needs of the diocese as the bishop may direct.

29. Among the close assistants of the bishop are those priests to whom he has entrusted a pastoral task, or an apostolate, which is of a supraparochial nature, whether in a special area of the diocese, or among special groups of the faithful, or some other special type of work.

Extremely valuable assistance is rendered by those priests to whom the bishop entrusts various works of the apostolate, whether it be in schools or in other institutions or associations. Likewise, those priests who are engaged in work of a supradiocesan nature are especially recommended to the special care of the bishop in whose diocese they live because they perform outstanding work in the apostolate.

30. Pastors are in a very special way the fellow workers of the bishop; the care of souls in a particular part of the diocese is entrusted to them as individual shepherds under the authority of the bishop.

(a) In the exercise of this charge, pastors and their assistants should carry out their office of teaching, sanctifying and governing in such a manner that the faithful and the parish communities become truly conscious of themselves as members both of the diocese and of the whole universal Church. For this reason they should collaborate with other pastors, as well as with those priests who exercise a pastoral office in the area (e.g., vicars forane or deans) or who are engaged in activities of a supraparochial nature, so that there will be no lack of unity in the pastoral work of the diocese, thus making that work more effective.

The care of souls should be infused by a missionary spirit so that it extends, in a suitable manner, to everyone living in the parish. If, however, pastors are unable to make contact with certain groups of people, they should seek the aid of others, even lay people, who could help them in their apostolate.

To make the care of souls more effective, a community life for priests, especially priests of the same parish, is strongly recommended. This would promote apostolic activity and give the faithful an example of charity and unity.

(b) In carrying out the office of teacher, it is the duty of pastors to preach the Word of God to all the faithful so that, rooted in charity and hope, they might grow in Christ, and so that the Christian community might bear that witness to charity recommended by the Lord.[32] They should also lead the faithful by catechetical instruction to a full knowledge of the mystery of salvation, a knowledge that is adapted to their age. In imparting this instruction they should seek the assistance not only of religious, but also of the laity, and establish a Confraternity of Christian Doctrine.

In accomplishing the work of sanctification, pastors should ensure that the celebration of the eucharistic sacrifice is the center and summit of the whole life of the Christian community. They should labor so that the faithful might be nourished with spiritual food by the devout and frequent reception of the sacraments and by attentive and active participation in the liturgy. They should be mindful of how greatly the sacrament of penance contributes to fostering a Christian life, and therefore make themselves easily available for hearing the confessions of the faithful. If necessary they should seek the assistance of other priests who speak different languages.

In fulfilling the office of shepherd, pastors should especially make a sincere effort to know their own flock. Since they are the servants of all the faithful, they should foster the growth of the Christian life in each of them singly, as well as in families, in associations (especially those engaged in the apostolate) and in the whole parish community. They should therefore visit homes and schools insofar as it is required by their pastoral duty; they should take a very special interest in adolescents and young people; they should treat the poor and sick with paternal charity; they should have a special concern for workers and encourage the faithful to participate in the activities of the apostolate.

---

[32] Cf. Jn. 13, 35.

(c) Curates, as the assistants of the pastor, daily render valuable and effective assistance by the exercise of their pastoral ministry under his authority. Therefore, there should always be mutual friendship, charity and respect between the pastor and his curates; they should aid each other by advice, assistance and example, providing for the welfare of the parish in unity and by a common effort.

31. In forming a judgment on the suitability of a priest for the administration of any parish, the bishop should take account not only of his knowledge of doctrine, but also of his piety, apostolic zeal and other gifts and qualities which are necessary for the proper exercise of the care of souls.

Since the whole purpose of the pastoral office is the good of souls, in order that the bishop might more easily and suitably provide for parishes, all rights, whether general or particular, of presentation, nomination or reservation, as well as the right of *concursus* wherever it exists, are to be suppressed. The rights of religious, however, must be safeguarded.

Pastors should enjoy in their own parish that stability in office which is required for the good of souls. Therefore, the distinction between removable and irremovable parish priests is abolished and the method to be used in transferring and removing pastors is to be revised and simplified so that the bishop, while maintaining natural and canonical equity, might be better able to provide for the good of souls.

Pastors who, because of old age or some other serious reason, are unable to effectively and fruitfully fulfill their offices, are strongly urged to resign either on their own accord or when invited to do so by the bishop. The bishop should provide for the proper support of those who resign.

32. Finally, the salvation of souls should be the ultimate criterion in determining or reconsidering the erection or suppression of parishes or any other changes which the bishop may make on his own authority.

33. All religious—and in regard to what follows, members of other institutes who profess the evangelical counsels are considered to be religious—have the duty, each according his own vocation, to work strenuously and zealously for the building up and the increase of the whole body of Christ and for the good of particular Churches.

They are obliged to work for these ends primarily by prayer, by works of penance and by the example of their lives, and the Council strongly urges them to grow continually in their appreciation and zeal for these means. They should give themselves more fully to the external works of the apostolate, taking into account the special character of each order.

34. Religious priests, consecrated in the priestly office so that they, too, might be the prudent fellow workers of the episcopal order, can today be of even greater assistance to the bishops because of the growing needs of souls. Therefore, they must be said to belong to the clergy of the diocese in a very real way, insofar as, under the authority of the bishop, they share in the care of souls and the work of the apostolate.

Other religious, both men and women, who are also in a special way members of the diocesan family, are a tremendous help to the hierarchy, and as time goes by and the demands of the apostolate increase, they can and should provide more and more help.

35. In order that the works of the apostolate might be harmoniously carried out in each diocese

and the unity of diocesan discipline safeguarded, the following basic principles are laid down:

(a) Since the bishops are the successors of the apostles, all religious should behave toward them with deep reverence and respect. Whenever they are lawfully called upon to carry out works of the apostolate, they should perform their tasks as active and obedient helpers of the bishop.[33] Indeed, religious should respond promptly and loyally to the requests and wishes of bishops in order that they might undertake a greater share in the work of human salvation; however, they should act in accordance with the character and constitutions of their community, which, if need be, should be adapted to this end according to the principles of this present conciliar Decree.

Especially in view of the urgent needs of souls and the shortage of diocesan clergy, religious communities which are not dedicated to a purely contemplative life may be called upon by bishops to help in the various pastoral ministries; the special character of each community should, however, be taken into account. Superiors should do their utmost to see that this assistance is given, even, if necessary, by taking over parishes temporarily.

(b) Religious who work in the apostolate should be imbued with the spirit of their own order; they should remain faithful to the observance of their rule and submissive to their own superiors. Bishops should not neglect to remind them of this obligation.

(c) Exemption, by which religious are attached to the pope or some other ecclesiastical authority and removed from the jurisdiction of bish-

[33] Cf. Pius XII, Allocution of Dec. 8, 1950: *A.A.S.* 43 (1951), p. 28; cf. also Paul VI, Allocution of May 23, 1964: *A.A.S.* 56 (1964), p. 571.

ops, mainly concerns the internal running of the institute so that everything in it might be better arranged and organized, and so that the growth and perfection of religious life might be fostered.[34] Exemption also permits the pope to use religious for the good of the whole Church [35] and other ecclesiastical authorities to use them for the good of the Churches under their jurisdiction.

This exemption, however, does not prevent the religious in each diocese from being subject to the jurisdiction of the bishop in accordance with the law, insofar as it is demanded for the exercise of the pastoral office and for a properly organized care of souls.[36]

(d) All religious, both exempt and non-exempt, are subject to the authority of local ordinaries in all that concerns the public exercise of divine worship (without detriment, however, to differences of rite), the care of souls, preaching to the people, the religious and moral education of the faithful (especially children), catechetical instruction and liturgical formation, the behavior proper to the clerical state and the various activities which are involved in the exercise of the sacred apostolate. Catholic schools conducted by religious are also subject to the local ordinaries as regards their general organization and supervision, without, however, infringing on the rights of religious in the running of them. Likewise, religious are bound to observe all those things which councils or conferences of bishops lawfully prescribe for observance by all.

---

[34] Cf. Leo XIII, Apostolic Constitution *Romanos pontifices,* May 8, 1881: *Acta Leonis XIII,* Vol. 2 (1882), p. 234.

[35] Cf. Paul VI, Allocution of May 23, 1964: *A.A.S.* 56 (1965), pp. 570-71.

[36] Cf. Pius XII, Allocution of Dec. 8, 1950, *loc. cit.*

(e) There should be organized cooperation between the different religious communities, and between those communities and the diocesan clergy. There should be a very close coordination of all apostolic works and activities; this will greatly depend on a supernatural attitude of mind and heart which is rooted and founded in charity. It pertains to the Holy See to bring about this coordination in the Church as a whole, to bishops in their own dioceses and to patriarchal synods and episcopal conferences in their own territory.

Before religious undertake works of the apostolate, bishops, or conferences of bishops, and religious superiors, or conferences of major superiors, should first discuss the matter together.

(f) To promote harmonious and fruitful relations between bishops and religious, both bishops and religious superiors should come together at set times, and as often as may seem necessary, to discuss matters related to the exercise of the apostolate in their territory.

Study-Club Questions

1. How should bishops enter into dialogue with society?

2. Bishops should dedicate themselves to their apostolic office as witnesses of Christ before all men. Explain.

3. Mention and briefly discuss the value of three means available today for proclaiming Christian doctrine.

4. Which members of the Church require catechetical instruction? Explain.

5. What can bishops do today to help organize, promote and guard the liturgical life of the Church?

6. What can bishops do to become more acquainted with the people they serve?

7. What can bishops do to regulate their own lives in a way that is in keeping with the needs of the times?

8. What can bishops do to better provide for the spiritual, intellectual and material welfare of priests?

9. What can bishops do to better provide for the spiritual, intellectual and material welfare of lay people?

10. Why are the faithful obliged to participate in apostolic work?

11. By devoting themselves to the spiritual care of their flock, bishops truly contribute to social and civil progress. Explain.

12. Why should some bishops resign from their office?

13. Mention some ways in which diocesan boundaries could be revised.

14. What is the first thing to be safeguarded in revising diocesan boundaries? Explain.

15. Why do diocesan priests have the principal role in the care of souls?

16. Mention and briefly discuss two supraparochial apostolates in your diocese.

17. What does this Decree say about the duties of pastors?

18. What does this Decree say about the duties of parish priests?

19. How should religious orders participate in the work of a diocese?

20. What would you suggest for a more fruitful and harmonious relationship between bishops and religious communities?

CHAPTER III

ON BISHOPS COLLABORATING FOR THE COMMON GOOD OF MANY CHURCHES

I. Synods, Particular Councils and Episcopal Conferences

36. From the very early centuries of the Church, bishops, although placed at the head of individual churches, have been united in fraternal charity. Moved by zeal for the universal mission entrusted to the apostles, they have combined their energies and purposes to promote both the common good and the good of individual Churches. For this reason, synods, provincial councils, and finally plenary councils were established in which the bishops laid down a common norm to be followed by the individual churches in teaching the truths of the faith and in organizing ecclesiastical discipline.

This sacred ecumenical Council desires that the venerable institutions of synods and councils should once again flourish so that the growth of the faith and the maintainance of discipline in the various churches might be more suitably and effectively provided for in accordance with the circumstances of the times.

37. Today, especially, it often happens that bishops cannot adequately or fruitfully fulfill their office unless they increasingly work in greater harmony with other bishops and cooperate more

closely with them. Since episcopal conferences, already established in many countries, have provided clear evidence of being a means to a more fruitful apostolate, this sacred Synod considers that it would be extremely useful if, throughout the world, the bishops of the same nation or region were to come together in one body, meeting at fixed times, so that by an exchange of views there might be a holy union of forces for the common good to the Churches.

38. Therefore, with regard to episcopal conferences the following is decreed:

(a) The episcopal conference is a type of body in which the bishops of a particular nation or region exercise their pastoral office together in order to increase the good which the Church offers to men, especially by forms and methods of the apostolate which are suitably adapted to the particular circumstances of the age.

(b) With the exception of vicars general, the following are members of the episcopal conferences: all local ordinaries of whatever rite, coadjutor and auxiliary bishops, and other titular bishops who perform some special task assigned to them by the Holy See or by episcopal conferences. Other titular bishops are not *de iure* members of the conference, nor are papal legates because of the special office which they hold in the territory.

Local ordinaries and coadjutors have a deliberative vote. Auxiliaries and other bishops who have a right to be present at the conference shall be accorded a deliberative or consultative vote according as is determined by the statutes of the conference.

(c) Each episcopal conference shall draw up its own statutes which must be approved by the Holy See. In these statutes they shall establish, among other things, those offices which are necessary for the more effective attainment of the end in view—e.g., they shall provide for a permanent committee of bishops, episcopal commissions, and a general secretary.

(d) Decisions of episcopal conferences, which have been lawfully passed by at least two-thirds of the bishops who have a deliberative vote in the conference, and which have been approved by the Holy See, are legally binding only in those cases which are laid down by common law, or prescribed by a special decree of the Holy See, acting either on its own (*motu proprio*) or at the request of the conference itself.

(e) Where it is demanded by special circumstances, the bishops of a number of nations may, with the approval of the Holy See, form a single conference. Contact between episcopal conferences of different nations should be encouraged in order to ensure and promote even greater benefits.

(f) It is strongly recommended that the bishops of the Oriental Churches, in promoting the discipline of their own particular Churches in synods, and in fostering more effectively the good of religion, also concern themselves with the common good of the whole territory in which there may be many Churches of different rites. They should exchange views at gatherings in which the different rites would come together in accordance with norms which should be drawn up by the competent authority.

II. Boundaries of Ecclesiastical Provinces and the Erection of Ecclesiastical Regions

39. The good of souls demands not only a suitable delimitation of dioceses, but also of ecclesias-

tical provinces. It suggests the creation of ecclesiastical provinces so that the needs of the apostolate might be better served in a manner that is in keeping with local circumstances and social conditions. In this way the relationship of bishops with each other, with their metropolitans, and with other bishops of the same nation, will become easier and more fruitful, as will also the relationship of bishops with the civil authorities.

40. Therefore, in order that these ends might be attained, this sacred Synod decrees as follows:

(a) The boundaries of ecclesiastical provinces should be revised at an early date, and the rights and privileges of metropolitans should be defined by new and suitable regulations.

(b) As a general rule, all dioceses and other territorial divisions which by law are equivalent to dioceses should be attached to some ecclesiastical province. Therefore, those dioceses which at present are immediately subject to the Holy See and not united with any other diocese should be brought together to form a new ecclesiastical province, if that is possible, or else attached to whatever province is nearest or most convenient. They should be subject to the metropolitan jurisdiction of the archbishop in accordance with common law.

(c) Wherever it appears useful, ecclesiastical provinces should be combined into ecclesiastical regions whose organization is to be determined by law.

41. It is desirable that this question of the delimitation of provinces and the creation of new regions should be examined by the competent episcopal conferences, in accordance with the norms already laid down in nn. 23 and 24, and that their suggestions and proposals should be placed before the Holy See.

III. Bishops Engaged in Interdiocesan Work

42. Since pastoral needs increasingly require that certain pastoral tasks be jointly directed and organized, it is desirable that some offices be established for the common service of all or several of the dioceses in a particular region or country, and possibly entrusted to a bishop.

This sacred Synod recommends that between the prelates or bishops exercising these offices and the diocesan bishops and episcopal conferences there should be at all times fraternal unity and harmony of purpose in the exercise of this pastoral ministry, the nature of which should be defined by common law.

43. Because of the particular circumstances of their lives, the spiritual care of military personnel demands very special attention; therefore, whenever it is possible, a special vicariate for the armed forces should be established in each country. Both vicar and chaplains should give themselves unreservedly to this difficult work in harmonious cooperation with the diocesan bishops.[37]

Therefore, the diocesan bishops should provide the vicar for the armed forces with a sufficient number of suitable priests for this important work, and they should likewise support those undertakings

[37] Cf. Sacred Consistorial Congregation, *Instruction to Military Vicars,* April 23, 1951: *A.A.S.* 43 (1951), pp. 562-65; *Formula To Be Followed for Establishing a Military Vicariate,* Oct. 20, 1956: *A.A.S.* 49 (1957), pp. 150-63; *Decree on "Ad Limina" Visits of Military Vicars,* Feb. 28, 1959: *A.A.S.* 51 (1959), pp. 272-74; *Decree on the Granting of Faculties for Confessions to Military Chaplains,* Nov. 27, 1960: *A.A.S.* 53 (1961), pp. 49-50. Also cf Sacred Congregation of Religious, *Instruction on Religious Military Chaplains,* Feb. 2, 1955: *A.A.S.* 47 (1955), pp. 93-97.

which are aimed at promoting the spiritual welfare of military personnel.[38]

General Directive

44. This most sacred Synod decrees that, in the revision of the Code of Canon Law, suitable laws be drafted in accordance with the principles laid down in this Decree; these laws should also take into account the observations put forward by the commissions and the conciliar fathers.

This Synod likewise decrees that general directories on the care of souls should be prepared for the use of both bishops and parish priests which would provide them with reliable rules for carrying out their pastoral office more easily and effectively.

A special directory should also be prepared on the pastoral care of particular groups of the faithful according to the different circumstances of each country or region. There should also be a directory on the catechetical instruction of the Christian people which would consider the fundamental principles and structure of such instruction and the preparation of books on the subject. In the preparation of these directories the observations put forward by both the commissions and the conciliar fathers should be taken into account.

* * *

Each and every point stated in this Declaration has satisfied the fathers of the sacred Council. And we, by the authority bestowed on us by Christ, to-

---

[38] Cf. Sacred Consistorial Congregation, *Letter to the Cardinals, Archbishops, Bishops and Other Ordinaries of Spanish-Speaking Nations,* June 21, 1951: *A.A.S.* 43 (1951), p. 566.

gether with the venerable fathers, approve it in the Holy Spirit, we decree it and we enact it; and we order the promulgation, to God's glory, of what has been enacted synodically.

Rome, in St. Peter's Basilica, October 28, 1965

Paul, Bishop of the Catholic Church
(The Fathers' signatures follow)

Study-Club Questions

1. Why should a diocesan bishop concern himself with the problems of another diocese?

2. What is the purpose of an episcopal conference?

3. What would be the value of episcopal conferences between a number of nations?

4. What does this Decree say about the bishops of Oriental churches?

5. Mention some apostolic work that requires inter-diocesan cooperation.

6. Mention some pastoral problems of bishops that this Decree does not discuss.

7. Why does Vatican Council II desire that synods and councils should flourish again in the Church?

8. Bishops cannot adequately fulfill their office unless they work in greater harmony with other bishops. Explain.

9. Who should determine the statutes of episcopal conferences? Explain.

10. What can bishops do to further the spiritual welfare of military personnel?

11. Who may participate in episcopal conferences?

12. Mention three ways in which bishops can cooperate for the common good of many Churches.

13. How many directories does this Decree urge to be set up?

14. Mention some pastoral problems that should be considered by episcopal conferences in your area.

15. What is the difference between an episcopal province and a diocese?

16. What is an ecclesiastical region?

17. What is a provincial synod?

18. What does this Decree say about the Commission for the Revision of the Code of Canon Law?

19. Briefly discuss three major conclusions of this Decree.

20. What can you do to carry out the provisions of this Decree?